IMAGES
of America

FORT WORTH

ON THE COVER: In 1876, the year the railroad came to Fort Worth, the Tarrant County Courthouse burned, destroying virtually all county records. By late 1876, work started on the beautiful cruciform courthouse shown here, with completion in 1878 when this photograph was taken. By 1882, a growing population led to additional courtrooms on the third floor, with a long wing destroying the building's symmetry a few years later. Complete demolition made room for the current 1895 courthouse. Other buildings shown, from right to left, are the Tarrant House Hotel on the east side of the square, O.B. Langever, proprietor; Gus Canto Market, Canto and Stein; August Canto's Meat Market; and Zimmerman and Lee Bakery, which also sold fruits and candies. Behind the bakery is the old Masonic lodge, and behind Gus Canto Market are chimneys and rooftops of homes. A five-rail wood fence keeps animals away from the courthouse. The older courthouse allowed livestock on the ground floor. In the foreground, nearly 50 wagons and horses with some 60 men and boys and countless bales of cotton marked with initials stand ready for market. It appears City Marshal Timothy Isaiah Courtright, who served from 1876 to 1879 and was later killed in a gunfight on the streets of Fort Worth by Luke Short, is standing on a bale with two other men at left center. (Courtesy of Dr. Harold V. Johnson III Collection, Tarrant County Archives.)

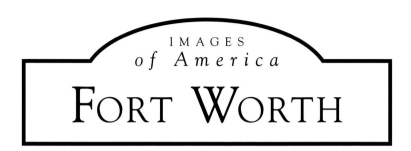

IMAGES
of America

FORT WORTH

Dawn Youngblood, PhD

ARCADIA
PUBLISHING

Published by Arcadia Publishing
Charleston, South Carolina

Printed in the United States of America

Library of Congress Control Number: 2019941208

For all general information, please contact Arcadia Publishing:
Telephone 843-853-2070
Fax 843-853-0044
E-mail sales@arcadiapublishing.com
For customer service and orders:
Toll-Free 1-888-313-2665

Visit us on the Internet at www.arcadiapublishing.com

Out Where the West Begins

Out where the handclasp's a little stronger,
Out where the smile dwells a little longer,
That's where the West begins;

Out where the sun is a little brighter,
Where the snows that fall are a trifle whiter,
Where the bonds of home are a wee bit tighter,
That's where the West begins.

Out where the skies are a trifle bluer,
Out where the friendship's a little truer,
That's where the West begins;

Out where a fresher breeze is blowing,
Where there's laughter in every streamlet flowing,
Where there's more of reaping and less of sowing,
That's where the West begins.

Out where the world is in the making,
Where fewer hearts in despair are aching,
That's where the West begins.

Where there's more of singing and less of sighing,
Where there's more of giving and less of buying,
Where a man makes a friend without half trying,
That's where the West begins.
—Arthur Chapman, 1917

CONTENTS

ACKNOWLEDGMENTS

Deep gratitude is extended to all who have worked to preserve the history of Fort Worth, and particularly all who have contributed to the Tarrant County Archives. Top of my list is award-winning preservationist and collector Dalton Hoffman, who has volunteered without fail at the Tarrant County Archives in downtown Fort Worth since 2011. Many of the images shown here were collected by him. Next, a heartfelt thank-you goes to all staff and volunteers at the Tarrant County Archives, particularly project archivist Amanda Milian, who scanned the images.

Special gratitude is extended to Richard F. Selcer, Scott Barker, Dalton Hoffman, Edwin Youngblood, and Amanda Milian for graciously commenting following careful and insightful consideration of each page. I am much indebted for your kindness.

In selecting the photographs, several considerations were used. First, all are from the Tarrant County Archives, which I have directed for almost a decade. These are the images with which I have become intimately familiar. This includes selections from our nearly 700 named collections. Second, I considered what images have already been used in past local history books so that this new album would be both accessible and fresh. Third, I have worked to feature a balance of intimate portraits, street scenes, and depictions of single structures with stories to tell. Many of the images in this book have never been published before, offering a fresh view of the history of Fort Worth. Many of the images in the first chapter are new acquisitions of the archives through a generous gift from the Fash Foundation. All identifications of persons and places in those images are taken at face value as provided in the accession paperwork.

If you are interested in researching or preserving Fort Worth and Tarrant County history, we are here for you. Find us online at www.tarrantcounty.com or call us at 817-884-3272.

All images in this book are from the Tarrant County Archives, Fort Worth, Texas.

LIST OF DONORS TO THE TARRANT COUNTY ARCHIVES

Robert G. Adams
Luis Aguila
Sam V. Akins
Tyler Alberts
Alcon Laboratories
Melanie Alexander
Dee Allen
Ellen Allen
Frances Allen
Katherine Allen
Amon Carter Museum
Dick Anderson
Roger Anderson
James Archer
Arlington Historical Society
Ann Arnold
Mary Kathryn Hoaldridge Arnold
George N. Ashabranner
James P. Ashley
Ruth Augustine family
Jackie L. Autrey
Jerry D. Bailey
Barbara Baker
Jonathan Hamilton Baker
Joseph J. Ballard
Craig Baltzer
Mary Ann Baltzer
William J. Bardin
Joe P. Barentine II
Dee Barker
Scott Barker
Barbara Barnett
Charles P. Barnett
Effie Barton
Batts family (April Herrington)
Kathy Hamer Beck
Bedford Historical Foundation
Bill D. Benge
Joseph Bentley

Margaret Smith Berry
Beverly S. Bier
Peter G. Bilheimer
Birdville Association of Retired
    School Personnel
Birdville Baptist Church
Birdville Historical Society
Vicky Tremble Bland
Gary Blevins
Cirrus Bonneau
Don W. Boston
Edith & V.W. Boswell
Lorin Boswell Jr.
Margie B. Boswell
Clota Terrell Boykin
David Branch
Cynthia Brants
James Preston Brashear III
Brazos Productions
Britton Cemetery
Bess Smith Broderick
Elton Brooks
Mildred Brown
Tom Brown
Mae McRae Bruce
Jane Austin Bruckner
Jon S. Brumley family
John L. Bryan Jr.
Vickie Bryant
Larry Budanauro
Bob Bullock
Devore O. Burch
Lynn Burel
Stewart Burge
Mary F. Burgon
Betty Burns
Carolyn Burns
Marcell Burns
Sam Jerry Burns

Wayne Butler
Michael Byrnes
Sarah Calhoun
Paul Campbell
Weldon G. Cannon
Riley Cantrell
Joyce Pate Capper
Electra M. Carlin
Erik Carlson
Naomi Carrier
Burl Carrol
Frances Sells Cartright
Ty Cashion
Mark Cashman
Allan Cathey
Ahdel Chadwick
Pete Charlton
Gary Christopher
Dominick J. Cirincione
City of Bedford
City of Benbrook
City of Colleyville
City of Dalworthington Gardens
City of Fort Worth Aviation Dept.
City of Fort Worth Parks Dept.
City of Fort Worth Planning Dept.
City of Mansfield Planning Dept.
Floyd Clark
Josh Clark
Jennifer Clark
Vivan B. Cloyd
Pam Coburn
Tom F. Cockerell
Frances Cogburn
Thomas J. Cogdell
Barbara Coker
Judy Cole
Colleyville Historical Preservation
    Committee

Colleyville Sesquicentennial
  Book Committee
Colleyville Woman's Club
Mile Cochran
Colonial Country Club
Frances Colwell
Sam Connery
Billie Cooper
Raymond H. Copeland
Cynthia Ann McPeak Cox
Kerry Coy
Mary Crabb
Pen Cranz
Creative Arts Theatre & School
Roger C. Cripliver
Crosby County Historical Memorial
Keller Crowley
Wes Culwell
Evelyn Cushman
Dallas Public Library
Robert Dalton
Dalworthington Gardens Historical
  Committee
Louis Daniel
Shirley Daniel
John Darden family
Michael I. Darter
Daughters of the American
  Revolution, Six Flags Chapter
Bill Davis
Kenneth Davis
Link Davis
Mitzi Davis
J.C. Dawson
Glenn Day
Edith A. Deen
Samuel Alexander Denny/Jennings
  family
Ann Diamond
Walter Clay Dixson
Lisa Dodd
Jan Dolph
Mike Douglas
Betty Drewry
Caroline Dulle
Felix Dulle
Joe K. Dulle
Jane & Stephen Dunkelberg
Dunkin family
Johnny Dunlap
J.W. & Mary Gregory Dunlop
Dolores Dunn

Joyce B. Dunning
Katherine Backus Durbin
Ray Eller
Robert Dale Erickson
Bernice Evans
Celestine Evans
Jim Evans
Ronald W. Evans
Joye Evetts
Roy Falls
Family Services Inc.
Fancher family
Ann Ware Farmer
Evan S. Farrington III
Fash Foundation
Hon. Pat Ferchill
Dan Fergus
Donald Ferrier
Linda Ferrier
Michael Fielder
First Baptist Church of Smithfield
First National Bank of Fort Worth
First Presbyterian Church of Fort
  Worth
Jeffrey Fisler
Jim Fitzgerald
Bonnie Flanagan
Joe Forsythe
Fort Worth Aviation Museum
Fort Worth Convention & Visitors
  Bureau
Fort Worth Genealogical Society
Fort Worth Opera
Fort Worth Petroleum Club
  Historical Committee
Fort Worth Star-Telegram
Fort Worth Transportation Authority
Kristy Fortenberry
Kevin Foster
Elaine Fountain
Franklin County Historical
  Commission
Dr. John W. Freese
Jim Frisinger
Betty Fuller
David Fuqua
Kirk Gabbert
Duane Gage
Sharon Gammon (Arnold-
  Humphries)
Ben Gantt
Viola Gardner

Julia Kathryn Garrett
Joseph Gearheart
General de Polignac Camp, Sons
  of Confederate Veterans
Julia Gibbins
Beryl Gibson
Robert Gieb
Dolores Orgain Gilbert
Cecilia Gilbreath
John Edwin Glascow
Nada Goble
Scot Goddard
Margaret Chenault Goodrich
Anna Melissa Hogsett Gordon
Carol Gordon
Grapevine Convention & Visitors
  Bureau
Grapevine Historical Society
Sallie Harper Graves
Greater Fort Worth Board of Realtors
Eleanor Frances Green
Phillip Greenwall
Kathleen Gregory
Gary Guess
Emile Guidroz
Charles Gumm
Ben Guttery
Terrye Guy
Kathryn Johns Halbower
Jean Ann Selman Hall
Carol Hallaran
Trudi Hallaran
Robert C. Haltom
Orville Hancock
Janet Hargrove
Sharon Harkness
B. Douglas Harman
Gerald Hartman Jr.
Harriss family
Elton Harwell
Ruth Hastings
Gary L. Havard
Thomas Robert Havins
Ed F. Havran
Billie Henderson
Suzanne Henderson
Ria Hendrix
Mary Lou Herring
Trey Herring
Lowell Herzog
David Hester
Patricia Hilborn

Harry Max Hill
Dr. John Hill
Historic Fort Worth Inc.
Historic Preservation Council of Tarrant County
Historical Publishing Network
Kenneth W. Hobbs
Dalton Hoffman
Bill & Frances Hogue
Barney B. Holland Jr.
Billie Holmes
Clara Wallace and Robert P. Holmes
Holmes family
John W. Hooper
Rev. William Hoover
Bess Hornbeak
Carla Hoskins
Patsy Howard
O.M. Howell
Tad Howington
Hudson Cemetery Association
Weldon Hudson
William A. Hudson II
Roger D. Huffaker
Vance Hunt
Virgile P. Hutchinson
Wallace Hutchinson
Mercedes John Iglesias
Harriet Irby
Mary Jackson
Pam Jackson
Patricia Chadwell Jackson
Margaret McLean James
Trish James
Roland Jary
William R. Jary
Burton K. Jennings
Harold R. Jennings
Inez Davis Jewett
Jon P. Jezek
Harold V. Johnson III
J. Mitchell Johnson
Andrew S. Jones
Dora Davenport Jones
Jan Lynn Jones
Richard Davenport Jones
David Kaiser
Bruce Kalbach
Keller State Bank
George F. Kent family
KERA (North Texas Public Broadcasting)

Key family
Garren King
Steve M. King
Beth Kisor
Susan Allen Kline
Kent Knudson
Emmit Koelle
Paul Koeppe
Janie Kruit
Mary Daggett Lake
Maurice Lambert
Harold Landers
David Lanier
Susan Layne
E. Brett Lea
Bill L. Leary
Debbie LeBlanc
Rufus Lester Leggett
Marty Leonard
Alice Marie Shannon Lewis
Dave Lieber
Lynn Ligon
LINC North Texas
Lipscomb family
Howard Livingston
J. Carter Llewellen
Jerry J. Lobdill
Oscar Lochridge
Howard M. Lock
Log Cabin Village
Barbara Logan
Hazel M. Lowrance
Russell Lowrance
Wayne Ludwig
William F. Ludwig
David Lynn
Anne Lyon
G.K. Maenius
Werner Magnus
Mike Mandel
Jean Manning
Mary Ann Manning
Mansfield Historical Society
Helen McKelvey Markgraf
Doyle Marshall
Cy Martin
Martin family
Marvin Martin
Peggy Martindale
William A. Massad
Frank Masters
Charles & Jean Matney

David & Donna Matney
Morris Matson
Carrol & Virginia Mathews
Judy Mauldin
Craig Maxwell
Leslie Ligon McClure
Megan Davis McConnell
Jane McCray
James McCreight
Michael S. McDermott
Kate McDonald
Eula McDuff
Mary McEvers
Grey McGown
Laura McGown
Quentin McGown IV
Morgan M. McGregor
Linda McKenzie
Madeline Williams McLain
Barbara McLane
Rogers McLane
Margaret McLean
Jim McLean
Rosalie McLeod
Harold McPeak
Howard McPeak
John A. Mead
Alan Meeker
Bo Meeks
J.M. Merrill
Frank Mesa Jr.
Mary Micio
Mid-Cities Genealogical Society
Amanda Milian
Jan Evans Miller
Judge Billy Mills
Minters Chapel Cemetery Association
Jerry D. Minton family
Kathy Misek
Leon Mitchell
Randall Moir
Judy Reid Molenburg
Michael J. Moncrief
Oscar Monnig
Emanuel F. Montes
J.A. Moore
James Bidault Moore
Abby Moran
Ben & Deanna Morgan
William Morrow & Co. Inc.
Joe Mulholland Jr.
Kathryn Murdock

Melody Muth-Smith
James Myrick
Beverly Nelms
Henry Newman
E. Vance Nichols
James Richard Nichols
Jeremy Dwight Nichols
Nickles family
Tom Niederauer
Jim Noah
North Fort Worth Community Arts Center
North Fort Worth Historical Society
North Richland Hills Historical Committee
North Richland Hills Public Library
Otto Oberle
Pearl Foster O'Donnell
Rush Olsen
Oral Histories of Fort Worth Inc.
May Owen
Paired Rail Railroad Publishing
Gladys Parchman
Vera Benton Parker
J'Nell Barnes Pate
Christina Patoski
Dr. Margaret Patoski
Michael Patterson
Joan Peterson Paulsen
David Pearson
Russell H. Pearson
Godfrey Pegues
Bill Perdue
Dr. Clay Perkins
Sandra Perry/Elliott family
Ted C. & Betty Scott Peters
Lolly Pinkston
Pioneer Rest Cemetery Association
Jo Pirtle
Jim Pitts
Helen Jennings Pomykal
Pope, Hardwick, Christie, Harrell, Schell, & Kelly LLP
Betty Porter
William A. Potter
Linda C. Pound
Caroline Powell
Marie Powell
Douglas Pritchett
Susan M. Pritchett
John Pugh
G.D. Pyeatt

Peggy Quinn
Simone C. De Santiago Ramos
Thelma Ray
Steve Reames
Vera Redding
Jack Reichenstein
Marcus T. Reiners
Audrey Remley
Dorothy Rencurrel
Nora Reves
Larry Reynolds
Grace Rhoden
Ann L. Rhodes Estate
Nikki Grote Rhodes
Royce Rhodes
Melvy Blue Rice
David L. Richards
Rosemary Rimbey
River Oaks Area Historical Society
Carol Roark
Chris Roberts
Lesbia Word Roberts
Tera Roberts
Kathy Robertson
Deputy Sheriff Rodrigo Robles
Dana Roe
Wayne A. Rohne
Rosen Heights Land Company
Dr. Charles A. Rush Jr.
Roy D. Russell
Mandy Saal
E.J. Sache
Saginaw Cemetery Association
St. Andrew's Episcopal Church, Fort Worth
Janet Saltsgiver
Linda Sanders/Backus family
Barry Sandlin
Gerald Saxon
Gregory C. Schadt
Jane Schlansker
Ruby Schmidt
Philip Eliot Schuab
Albert R. Schultz
Frances Merrill Scott
Karolyn McPeak Scott
Scroggins-Mills
Mildred C. Smith Searcy
Jerry Secrest
Richard F. Selcer
Sesquicentennial Committee, Richland Hills

Dolores D. Sety/ Darcy Sety
Joe Shannon
Trey Shannon
Glen Robert Shaw Jr.
Drusilla Cochran Sheldon
Ruby Thompson/Shemwell family
Maris Shepherd
Jamie Powell Sheppard
Linda Sherwood
Don Shiflet
Atha Loraine Simmons
Thomas Wall Simmons
Richard Don Simms
Paul Skoog
Ken Slade
Bennett Smith
Christie L. Smith
Harry E. & Jane K. Smith
John Hugh Smith
Juliet Ada George Smith
Karen Duay Smith
Lawanda & Jim Smith
Melvina Grunewald Smith
Sister Louise Smith
Southwestern Baptist Theological Seminary
Joyce Hudnall Sparks
Leslie Spoontz Jr.
Mildred Spratling
Rudy E. Stallings
Charles Stamps
Lela Standifer
John & Ruth Starr
Raymond M. Stateham
Fred R. Steffen
Theda & Uel Stephens Jr.
Stewart Tile Company
B.J. Stone
Ruth Reiter Stone
Joe Strain
John B. Strait
Donald and Virginia Strathdee
Ben F. Stroder
Mary Standard Stults
Doug Sutherland
John Tandy
Tarrant County
Tarrant County Archaeological Society
Tarrant County Bar Association
Tarrant County Black Historical & Genealogical Society

Tarrant County College, Northwest, Cornerstone Honors
Tarrant County Convention Center
Tarrant County Court of Appeals, Second District of Texas
Tarrant County Historic Preservation Council
Tarrant County Historical Commission
Tarrant County Historical Society
Tarrant County Junior College
Wyatt Teague
Telephone Pioneers of America, Fort Worth Life Members Club
Texas Archives Commission
Texas Christian University Press
Texas Christian University Special Collections, Mary Couts Burnett Library
Texas Dept. of Transportation
Texas Garden Clubs
Texas Health/Huguley Hospital
Texas Historical Commission
Texas Lakes Trail Region (Jill Campbell Jordan)
Harry T. Thatch
Willard Thomas
Camilla B. Thompson
J. Andy Thompson
Bill T. Thornton
Terry Timberlake
Vic Tinsley
Don Tipps
Trinity Episcopal Church
Pat & Ruthanna Truly
T.R. Turk
Raymond Mitchell Tucker
William A. Turner, United Daughters of the Confederacy
Deanna Tuttle
University Christian Church
US Army Corps of Engineers, Fort Worth District
U.S. Life Title Company (Rick Griffin)
Hon. Harold L. Valderas
Village Creek Archaeological Group
Evelyn Smith Hill Vogel
Ellen Timberlake Volz
Roger P. Waite
Ralph Walker
Karen Ann Walls

Tina Walls
Walsh Companies
Sharon Ward
Julie Elaine Reynolds Watson
Weatherford Public Library
Webb Historical Society
Jack Webb
Theresa Weddell
Hollace Ava Weiner
Arthur Weinman
Joseph Weisburg
Charles G. Welch
Wells Fargo
Westbrook Hotel
Dora Whalen
Gerald White
White Settlement Historical Society
Tom Wiederhold
Jack Wiesman
Wiggins family
Ernest J. Wilemon
W.D. Willhoite
Joe Williams
Lee Williams
Perry Williams
Phillip G. Williams
Victoria Williams
Thelma Williamson
Doyle Willis
Lissa Willis
Mary Ann Austin Willis
Marvin Wilson
Sharen Wilson
Cindy Wilson-Arrick
Willis C. Winters
Richard and Glenda Wittich
Woman's Wednesday Club of Fort Worth
Woodmen of the World
Walter C. Woodward
Kathy Barker Wreden
Hon. Jim Wright
Lallah Wright
Hon. Ron Wright
Jane Wiggins Gudgeon York
Charles Young
Judge Everett Young
Frances Young
Sharon Young
YMCA, Metropolitan Fort Worth
Dawn Youngblood
Edwin Johnston Youngblood

George Younkin
Jim M. Zadeh
Byron Zirkle

INTRODUCTION

GENESIS OF FORT WORTH

Just as a slender acorn holds all the future potential of a live oak, the genesis of Fort Worth held all its future character in a nutshell. Fort Worth has long been known as the city "Where the West Begins." There are several good reasons for this. Explaining those good reasons serves as an excellent introduction to Fort Worth's fascinating history. The reasons start with Sam Houston (commanding general, then president of the Republic of Texas, and later US senator, then governor of Texas), who signed a treaty with nine Native American tribes in 1843. The groups agreed to generally stay on opposite sides of a line in the vicinity of Fort Worth—so that the "Wild West" where "Indians" could be encountered would for some time have been west of Fort Worth. Differences in soil (less acidic/more alkaline), climate (more arid), plants (fewer trees outside of the river drainages), and animals (antelope and bison were rarely reported much east of Fort Worth) are also clear. In 1921, *Fort Worth Star-Telegram* publisher Amon G. Carter famously said, "Fort Worth is where the West begins, and Dallas is where the East peters out."

There is a simple explanation for why the fort called Worth was established where it was, when it was, and was named what it was: The Republic of Texas joined the United States in 1845; the United States entered into war with an offended Mexico in 1846. With that war won in 1848, the United States suddenly had troops returning from Mexico to Texas and a responsibility to protect those "Texians" who were now Americans. Gen. William Jenkins Worth (1794–1849) was assigned as commander of the newly created Department of Texas, with headquarters in San Antonio.

Fort Worth became the seat of Tarrant County in 1860. As you enjoy the photographs in this book, it may be handy to refer to the population numbers below. According to the US Census Bureau, Fort Worth was the fastest-growing city with more than 500,000 population between 2000 and 2010. During that decade, Fort Worth's total population increased by 206,512. This represents an average annual increase of approximately 20,650, and a growth rate of 3.9 percent per year. Tarrant County is the fifth-fastest growing county in the nation.

YEAR	TARRANT COUNTY POPULATION	FORT WORTH POPULATION
1850	664 (599 free, 65 slaves)	>100 (60 men stationed at the fort in 1853)
1860	6,020 (5,170 free, 850 slaves)	350 (175 during Civil War)
1870	5,788	500 estimated (approximately 4,000 in 1873)
1880	24,671	6,663
1890	41,142	23,076
1900	52,376	26,688
1910	108,572	73,312
1920	152,800	106,482
1930	197,553	163,447
1940	225,521	177,662
1950	361,253	278,778

Year	Tarrant County Population	Fort Worth Population
1960	538,495	356,268
1970	716,317	393,476
1980	860,880	385,141
1990	1,170,103	447,619
2000	1,446,219	534,694
2010	1,809,034	741,206

The leap in population reported by Fort Worth chronicler Buckley Boardman "B.B." Paddock (1844–1922) by 1873 was due to positive press. Thousands flocked to Fort Worth, including Paddock himself, in 1872–1873 because the town was selected as a route for the Texas and Pacific Railroad and was praised as the best place to be in northern Texas. In Paddock's own words from his 1906 booklet *Early Days in Fort Worth*:

Fort Worth first came into prominence in 1872, when Col. Thomas A. Scott who had come into the ownership and control of the Texas and Pacific Railway, in company with Col. John W. Forney, the editor and proprietor of the Chronicle of Philadelphia, made a trip across Texas for the purpose of selecting a route for this road across the State. Colonel Forney wrote voluminous letters to his paper describing in great detail what he saw and how he was impressed with the resources of the State. He afterwards wrote and published a pamphlet entitled "What I Saw in Texas" which had a wide circulation. In these letters and in the pamphlet, he had much to say about Fort Worth. In fact, he gave it more space than any other point in the State, and predicted for it a brilliant future. He did not hesitate to predict it would be the most prominent place in the northern part of the State. It being generally known that he was the guest of Colonel Scott on the trip it was quite natural that his readers should reach the conclusion that he reflected the opinion of the President of the Railway Company.

Early that year, the value of a corner lot might literally double overnight. Then, in the fall of 1873, came news that the railway might not make it after all; the English investor Jay Cooke & Co. had failed. Values declined as rapidly as they had grown, and many houses under construction were left half-finished. The rail reached as far as Eagle Ford, just west of Dallas, and there it was abandoned. Paddock bemoaned the timing: "Had the panic broken thirty days later so that it would have been practicable to have completed the road to Fort Worth before suspending operations, Dallas would have been a good county seat town instead of a thriving city and Fort Worth would today have been a city of a quarter million population." Paddock said "the grass literally grew in the streets. This was not a metaphor to indicate stagnation, but a doleful fact."

Most of the citizenry of Fort Worth moved to Dallas. One of these, attorney Robert A. Cowart, told the famous tale—in the *Dallas Herald* article from whence the nickname "Panther City" is derived—of a panther asleep in the streets of Fort Worth. For those who remained in Fort Worth, civic pride only grew, and the city was chartered March 1, 1873.

One

FROM FORT TO FIRE

1849–1876

Prior to "the fort called Worth," a few homesteads such as this 1840s dogtrot-style cabin dotted the landscape. In 1927, publisher and philanthropist Amon Carter moved Isaac Parker's cabin to his Shady Oaks Farm near Lake Worth, where the cabin is shown here dusted with snow. Upon Carter's death in 1955, the cabin was gifted and moved to Fort Worth's Log Cabin Village, where it remains with other early homes. It was to this cabin that Cynthia Ann Parker, a captive of the Comanche and mother to Chief Quanah Parker, was forcibly returned in 1860.

The location of Fort Worth was selected as the site for a military post in 1849 and named for Gen. William Jenkins Worth. Sadly, Worth, following decades in battle from the War of 1812 through the Mexican War ending in 1849, died of cholera in San Antonio that year. The name was chosen by post commander Ripley Allen Arnold (1817–1853), who had served under Worth. Above is a rendering of the fort by artist and historian William B. Potter. The John Gambrell family lived in the house pictured below on the old fort property, north of current Belknap at Houston, long after the fort closed, preserving this remnant for many years. The fort was constructed using a portable mechanical saw.

The daguerreotype at right, reputedly of Arnold with his bride, Catherine Bryant (1825–1894), is the only known image of the founder of Fort Worth. The couple wed in 1839 and had five children, but the 36-year-old father and husband was gunned down by his post surgeon at Fort Graham in 1853. Arnold was reinterred in the cemetery he founded upon the death of two of his children at Fort Worth: Sophia (1848–1850) and Willis (1838–1850), who was named after Ripley's father, soldier and minister Willis H. Arnold (1790–1835). Pictured below, Willis Arnold was president of the Pearlington Academy in Pearlington, Mississippi, where son Ripley was born and educated on the banks of the Pearl River. From there, Ripley Arnold attended West Point.

Lt. Samuel Starr served under Ripley Arnold for two years at Fort Worth until he left for Fort Mason on December 20, 1851, because a second line of forts was being established farther west. The first line, established in 1849, had Fort Worth as the northernmost point and Fort Graham just south of that, with a total of eight forts forming a line that reached to the Rio Grande. The second line farther west had Fort Belknap as the northernmost and Fort Mason west of Austin as one of 10 forts. When Lieutenant Starr made the move, he was married and had three daughters—with baby Jo having been born the month prior and little Annie the year before. Starr's wife, Eliza, and eldest daughter, Kate, must have had quite a lot on their minds during that winter move. Eliza Starr and Catherine Arnold became close, continuing their friendship via letters expressing the hardships and joys of their lives.

In this rare outdoor daguerreotype believed to have been taken in 1852, George Preston "Press" Farmer (1825–1892) is shown with 2nd US Dragoon Christian Bohrman seated on a mule-drawn wagon. French revolutionary, utopian leader, and trained daguerreotypist Adolphe Gouhenant (Gounah), who was present at the fort, may have created this and other images. Press Farmer, wife Jane Woody Farmer (1827–1895), and daughter Susan Ann (1847–1917) were Fort Worth's first family—settling on the bluff that is now downtown Fort Worth in May 1849, just three weeks prior to the arrival of Ripley Arnold. Arnold hired Farmer as the fort's supplier and freighter. Provisions such as vegetables, biscuits, button polish, and tobacco were brought by wagon from Houston along with meat and hay purchased from local settlers. The Farmer log cabin, the first house in Fort Worth, was torn down in 1888. It was located near the corner of what is now First and Henderson Streets, where apartments are now located.

Originally from England and a cabinetmaker by trade, Sgt. Abraham "Abe" Harris (1824–1915) served at the fort under Maj. Ripley Arnold as his sergeant major. He also helped build the officers' quarters and barracks. Harris mustered out of the service at the fort on January 20, 1852, and remained in what is now Tarrant County until his death. He married Margaret Conner, and the couple had five children. Harris continued his work in cabinetry, served as president of the Texas Association of Mexican War Veterans, and was hailed as the oldest surviving member of the original settlers who founded the city before he was buried in Pioneers Rest Cemetery near his old commander Ripley Arnold in 1915 at the age of 91. Throughout his adult life, he carried a family pocket Bible that is now housed at the Tarrant County Archives.

Pictured are two of the five Arnold children born to Catherine, who in 1839 married Ripley at the age of 14. Ripley may have had an additional son by a 20-year-old slave named Hagar. (The name Hagar is derived from the Biblical story of Abraham and Sarah: Hagar has a child before Sarah and is cast out once her mistress bears a son.) Shown are Arnold's daughters Florida (left) and Kate. Born in Louisiana, Katherine Ann (1843–1912) married Samuel J. Parker (1841–1876) of Marlin, Texas, and had four children—Willis, Flora Belle, Samuel Penn, and Anne Mary Parker. Flora Belle (1840–1868), also called Florida (the location of her birth), died in Marlin. Two years later, her husband, Confederate veteran Thomas Bolling Manlove, was listed as an editor in Waco with four-year-old daughter Molly.

Two daguerreotypes survive of Kate Arnold on horseback. The one above is believed to have been taken around 1852 and the one at right several years later on the East Coast. The fort had 52 horses, but the quartermaster kept another 22, for a total of 74. Each horse was fed eight quarts of grain and 14 pounds of hay daily. In the summer of 1852, Major Arnold had five horses auctioned off in Fort Worth, netting $127.39 for the Quartermaster Department. That would be the equivalent of $3,821.70 today.

Nannie Ripley Arnold Hanrick (1851–1875) was born at the fort called Worth. She married Edward C. Hanrick. The couple named their son after her father, Ripley Arnold Hanrick (1872–1953). Their daughter she named for herself—Nannie Hanrick. According to the *Baylor Bulletin Ex-Student's Directory* of 1920, daughter Nannie obtained a degree from Baylor University in 1896. She married Hugh M. Coleman and is buried at Elmwood Cemetery in Mineral Wells. Her son Ripley married Mary Louise Prescott, and they too named their son Ripley in 1904, so with Ripley Edward Hanrick the name was passed down until he died in 1969. He is buried at Oakwood Cemetery in Waco alongside his parents and grandparents. The rare ambrotype below is believed to depict the Fort Worth house used by the Arnold family in 1854 when the major's body was returned to Fort Worth for burial.

Dug and covered in 1857, Frenchman's Well was located where Taylor Street drops toward the Trinity River. Howard W. Peak, who was born in the garrison building of the fort in 1856 to the town's first doctor, Dr. Carroll Peak, said it was dug by Frenchman Alexander Barbier, who moved to Fort Worth from the failed La Réunion settlement—a utopian community formed in 1855 by French, Belgian, and Swiss colonists some 30 miles east of the fort. By 1860, most of the colonists had left La Réunion. While some moved to New Orleans and others returned to Europe, at least half settled elsewhere in Texas. The beehive well cover was moved to the courthouse grounds, where it was accidentally hit by a truck in the 1950s. Ollie Lake Burnett (1871–1966) had workmen gather up the pieces and reconstruct the well in her backyard at 4910 Crestline Road. In 2019, Brent Hyder, who grew up in that home, offered Frenchman's Well back to the county so that the public could again enjoy this treasured structure.

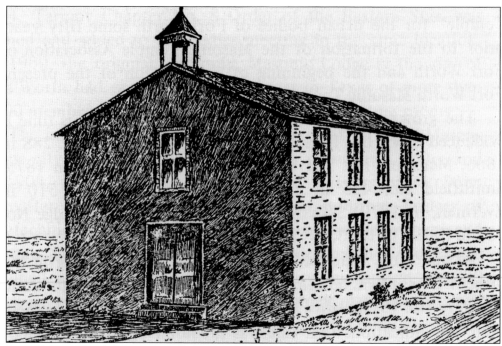

In 1854, Fort Worth Masonic Lodge No. 148 was founded. The two-story redbrick hall built by 1857 hosted Masonic functions upstairs, while school, church, and public meetings occurred on the ground level. In 1871, member Lawrence Steel provided the lodge his 1782 English-foundered bell that until then had graced his tavern. The Masonic Bell—now one of the most treasured relics in the city—was rung to announce stagecoach arrivals, fires, and the start of the school day.

Fort Worth's oldest surviving schoolhouse is Marine School, which served as a school between 1870 and 1905. In 1906, John Mulholland bought and moved it to 1309 North Commerce Street, where it was a residence, then abandoned. After the structure was condemned in 1991, the Friends of the Marine Schoolhouse rescued it; in 2003, Marine School became a beloved part of Log Cabin Village.

In 1873, the year Fort Worth was incorporated, Thomas Allen Tidball (1838–1899) arrived from Lafayette, Missouri, with his bride, Lelia Frances Arnold (1848–1945), and best friend, Linton C. Hutchins (1858–1908). That same year, Tidball, an experienced banker, and John B. Wilson established the first private bank in Fort Worth. Wilson, who supplied the main capital for starting the bank, returned to his home in Virginia the next year, whereupon Maj. K.M. Van Zandt (shown below), Maj. J.J. Jarvis, and John Peter Smith purchased controlling interest. In 1884, the bank received a charter as Fort Worth National Bank. The first location was a two-story building at 109 West Weatherford Street (a plaque is on the wall outside of Vaquero Coffee Shop). Thomas and Lelia had five children, all born in Fort Worth. Linton worked at the bank until he shot himself in the head at his desk at the age of 49. At the time, he was second vice president of the largest financial institution in the city. Both the Tidball and Hutchins families are buried at Fort Worth's Oakwood Cemetery.

During the Civil War era of the 1860s, Fort Worth's population dropped to 175. Food and money were in short supply, and previously prominent citizens, such as the first district attorney Dabney C. Dade, were forced to leave due to their refusal to take an oath to the Confederacy. In 1857, Dade had convinced Joe C. Terrell to settle in Fort Worth and set up a law office with him. Terrell returned to Fort Worth after fighting with the Confederacy, and became a longtime prominent citizen, but Dade took his leadership skills back to his home state of Missouri, where he became a state legislator. According to Terrell, the margin in the vote for secession in Tarrant County was narrow. A home guard was formed to protect remaining citizens from Kiowa and Comanche attacks. The last such raid, in 1867, was along the West Fork of the Trinity now covered by Eagle Mountain Lake. Shown is Charles Fain, a relative of Phillip Greenwall, who owned the Fort Worth Opera House.

Capt. Joe C. Terrell, in his *Reminiscences of the Early Days of Fort Worth*, wrote of the local young ladies, "It seems to me that the girls were prettier then. Their meek eyes and bright faces haunt me still." Upon setting up their two-room law office and living quarters, Terrell and Dade decided to teach Sunday school to meet the local girls. Apparently, it worked. While there are no photographs of the young ladies Terrell particularly admired, shown here is Leslie Stewart, whose family farm lay to the east, at a site now underneath Dallas Fort Worth International Airport. Her image seems to embody the spirit of Terrell's sentiments.

Two

FROM FIRE TO FIRE

1876–1909

This rare image of market day on the public square in 1877 shows business really picking up. Oliver Knight said 1877 Fort Worth "erupted into the wildest town in western Texas. By the hundreds came men and women who pictured Fort Worth, now the westernmost railhead, as a golden mecca." Cowboys, gunmen, buffalo hunters, gamblers, and dance hall girls descended on the town—along with churchgoing wealth-seekers and huddled masses. Supply could not keep up; some thousand lived in tents throughout the city. On a city block between Third and Fourth Streets on Main owned by K.M. Van Zandt, the city's first three-story building went up, the El Paso Hotel. The street corner visible at rear is Weatherford and Houston Streets, with the Daggett and Hatcher Store on the left.

Shown are the first portraits known to have been painted in Fort Worth—executed by French immigrant Eugene Pierrot in 1877. In keeping with the boomtown atmosphere, Pierrot created these paintings over faux finishes—hers over faux oak and his over faux marble—apparently touting his painting skills to those building saloons, hotels, and banks. He could make the bare wood surfaces appear to be marble or fine, quarter sawn oak. The subjects are Thomas Jefferson Jennings (1801–1881) and his wife, Sarah Hyde Mason Jennings (1816–1893). He served as Texas attorney general from 1852 to 1856. She patented 1,280 acres in Fort Worth and sent her son Hyde to manage her real estate interests. The Sarah Jennings survey is now the south side of downtown including city hall. In 1876, the year the Jennings men helped bring in the railroad, Sarah donated Block One to create the first public park. Later, the first public library would also sit upon her survey.

Within a decade, Fort Worth went from no telegraph line to trains, trolleys, lighted streets, and telephones. The first telephone and streetlights came to town in 1877, and the Yuma Stage in 1878. By 1880, the town was a nascent mix of civilization and wild west. Shown are Fort Worth city officials around 1880–1882. From left to right are (seated) Charles Garrison, Stuart Harrison (city secretary), Sam Farmer (marshal), John T. Brown (mayor), William Coleman, and Edward P. Maddox; (standing) W.T. Sands, Bill Neely, Ike Cantrell, Long Thomas, Bob Buchanan, Charley Scott, W.M. Rea, and Jack Riggle. In 1884, home delivery of mail began, and 1885 saw electric lighting.

Walter Ament Huffman (1846–1890) grew up the son of a local pioneer farmer but became Fort Worth's first homemade millionaire. At age 15, he volunteered to fight for the Confederacy. Upon his return in 1863, at age 17, he opened a dry goods store on the Courthouse Square. In 1877–1878, the city directories list him residing at the northeast corner of Second and Taylor Streets, with advertisements touting the W.A. Huffman Implement Co. The *Fort Worth Gazette* summed up his life: "There is no enterprise, business or social, to which he has not lent his influence . . . always in the vanguard of progress, Fort Worth today owes much of its advance to this master mind who, with a ken far exceeding that of common men, saw possibilities and possessed the courage to reach out for them." He was president of the North Side Railway and the board of trade and founder of the first electric company, treasurer for the Spring Palace, owner of the *Gazette*, and far more. Upon his death, his estate was valued at $1.4 million.

Native Americans spent time in Fort Worth as business partners and visitors in the 1880s. The most famous of these was Comanche chief Quanah Parker, son of Peta Nocona and Cynthia Ann Parker. His business partnership with rancher Dan Waggoner was of mutual benefit. In 1885, Parker was visiting with Waggoner's ranch foreman George T. Briggs when he returned to his room at the Pickwick, where Yellow Bear, who was traveling with him, was sleeping. Parker did not fully extinguish the gas light. He almost lost his life, and Yellow Bear did. In the rare photograph below by Augustus R. Mignon, who set up shop at 24 Main Street in Fort Worth in 1883, nine Native Americans pose with a family of four in front of a jacal-style and wooden building that appears to be the train depot.

Mignon also photographed this dynamic street scene in front of the Tarrant County Courthouse in 1883. A multiracial blend of well-dressed men conduct business on the square. This stone Tarrant County Courthouse completed in 1878 was already too small less than five years later, so by 1883, the original dome was replaced with the 16-foot-high mansard roof shown, allowing for well-ventilated rooms on the third story. The octagonal bell tower sported four 8-foot-diameter clock dials so that time could be told from any direction.

This 1886 image of the William Fletcher Lake Sr. (1850–1909) home at 605 East Bluff Street displays a sense of domestic tranquility. Note the third-story room from which fantastic views could be enjoyed. Lake came to Fort Worth during the cattle drive days in 1875 and engaged in the hardware business. He promoted the railroad coming to town and was instrumental in building it. Son Will Lake Jr. (1876–1953) continued the family business and married Mary Daggett (1880–1955), who was instrumental in forming the Fort Worth Botanic Gardens. The Daggett home was also on Bluff Street, and was the location of the elder W.F. Lake's funeral.

After a nomadic existence on the western frontier, Luke Lamar Short (1854–1893) spent the last 10 years of his life in Fort Worth. Growing up in Montague County, Short learned to shoot, ride, and throw a lariat. He worked as a cowboy, buffalo hunter, and US Army scout. Short took up the gambling life in the boomtowns of the West. In Tombstone, he killed a man. In 1883, he became part owner of the White Elephant Saloon at 310 Main Street, Fort Worth. In a legendary gunfight, Short killed lawman Timothy Isiah "Longhaired Jim" Courtright (1845–1887). The next month, he married Harriet Beatrice "Hattie" Buck (1863–1912). Bat Masterson wrote a 1907 account of Short's life as a "dandy gunfighter" and recalled Short as "one of the best-hearted men who ever lived." A Fort Worth minister once said, "I am proud to know Luke Short. Many a widow has been fed and many an orphan clothed in this city through the generosity of this man, who is in the eyes of many an outcast and a stranger."

Yellowstone Kit was an "Indian doctor" of mixed descent who promoted his wares on the streets of Fort Worth and created a sensation at the Texas Spring Palace. This portrait was taken at J.F. Daniel Studios, 610 Houston Street, Fort Worth, a couple of blocks from where Kit performed. In May 1890, the *Gazette* reported: "All over the South Kit is well known. . . . The entertainments given at his tent, corner Fifth and Houston streets, are refined, chaste, and he is patronized by the best of people. Good order is strictly maintained, and it is the current comment that Kit's tent is as well conducted as any church. Kit is a plain talker and although his truths are driven home, it does one good to listen to his scathing criticisms of some public men in high places. Rough and unshod he travels the road to truth, and has gained the friendship of all bankers, merchants, and rich men."

The Texas Spring Palace was constructed in 1889—and a larger version in 1890, near where Main Street intersects Lancaster Avenue—to bring national focus on the productivity of Texas. The festive concept was the idea of Gen. Robert A. Cameron of the Fort Worth and Denver Railway. City and railroad leaders invited each county in the state to participate by displaying its natural resources, art, crops, and products in a grandiose exhibit hall that was longer than a football field. The hall, designed by A.A. Messer (1863–1934), was a dizzying blend of Victorian and Asian styles and constructed of highly flammable materials, including dried corn and wheat amply fastened to interior and exterior surfaces. The palace hosted exhibits, dramatic performances, bands, balls, and demonstrations. Fire rapidly destroyed the structure on May 30, 1890. While many were injured, Englishman Alfred S. Hayne (1849–1890), who rescued others from the fire, was the only one to die. Valuable works of art and history on display were destroyed. The image below shows the Spring Palace from downtown. St. Patrick's Cathedral can be seen under construction on the right.

In this rare interior photograph of the Spring Palace, a band is ready to perform. The engraved stone at left reads, "W.F. Sommerville, Gen. R.A. Cameron, Directors General; E.O. Allen, Decorator."

The N.E. Grammer drugstore, owned by Nathaniel Grammer (1863–1911), moved to Main and Weatherford Streets in Fort Worth five years prior. His older brother, Dr. Robert Grammer (1861–1914) had an office in the same building. Grammer's grew to be the largest and most modern drugstore in the city. The year after settling in Fort Worth, Nathaniel Grammer married Lula Whatley (1868–1952). They had five children, with four boys surviving into adulthood. The later Grammer family residence, at 2232 College Street in Fairmount, stands today.

William Fife Sommerville (1848–1890) arrived from Scotland in 1882 as assistant manager of the Matador Land and Cattle Company's Fort Worth office. He helped form the first mortgage company in Fort Worth and served on the board of directors of the Fort Worth and Denver City Railway as well as being president of the Fort Worth Musical Union and 1890 governor general of the Texas Spring Palace. He died in an accident at his home on Penn Street involving a fall from a windmill platform onto the picket fence while his wife, Mary, and son Alfred were visiting England. To honor him, the chamber of commerce building was cloaked in black bunting for 30 days. Sommerville took the photograph below of Mary and Alfred with friends in the yard, providing a rare image of the 1882 Fort Worth skyline.

As the population of Tarrant County surpassed 40,000, the 1883 courthouse proved too small. It was demolished and replaced by the far grander 1895 courthouse shown here. Designed by Gunn & Curtis in 1893 and built by the Probst Construction Company of Chicago, this Texas granite building, in Renaissance Revival style, resembles the Texas Capitol, but with a clock tower instead of a dome. Citizens considered the $408,840 cost so extravagant that a new County Commissioners Court was elected in 1894. Public opinion turned, however, and the courthouse soon became a source of pride. Preserving it remains a priority of the county to this day. In 2020, its 125th anniversary will be celebrated.

Walter Maddox (1844–1910), the eldest of five brothers, arrived in Fort Worth with bride Sarah Hightower (1847–1924) and baby Rosa (1871–1906) in 1873 riding a wagon with two good horses. After running a livery stable for eight years, Maddox served three terms as sheriff (1880–1886), then worked in real estate and the furniture business. Brother Robert Maddox (1849–1907) served as tax assessor for the city in the 1870s. In 1890, he helped build the first permanent stockyards. Both brothers were listed at times among the highest taxpayers in the city. Brothers Benjamin, Seaborn, and Edward also followed Walter to Fort Worth. The men in this large family held several posts in law enforcement.

This beautiful and rare image intriguingly labeled "adopted daughter of Rachel" dates to 1896–1899 based on the Swartz Studio address of 705 Main Street. The young lady's story is unknown, though her photograph is treasured.

After becoming one of the youngest captains in the Confederate forces, B.B. Paddock (1844–1922) married his Mississippi sweetheart Emmie Harper (1848–1926) in 1867. He studied law, then moved to Fort Worth in 1872. Paddock served as mayor (1892–1900), several terms as state representative, editor of the *Fort Worth Democrat* (1873–1881), and president of the Fort Worth and Rio Grande Railway (1885–1889). He helped create Fort Worth's first city fire department, was president of the Texas Spring Palace, and became one of Fort Worth's biggest boosters. The Paddock home, at 901 South Jennings Avenue, was first wood frame, then brick. Around 1934 the Paddock descendents donated the land, and a school gymnasium was built on the property. Emmie was a charter member of what remains the oldest continuous club in Fort Worth, the Woman's Wednesday Club, founded in 1889.

Men and children stand in front of the 1884 Tarrant County Jail on Belknap and Calhoun Streets east of the courthouse. The first jail was built in 1858 by Sheriff John York (1825–1861), who died of stab wounds while in office. Below, Tarrant County lawmen take a stance with weapons inside the old jail behind the courthouse around the time the infamous Butch Cassidy and the Sundance Kid were in town in 1900. The men are identified as Jesse Rudd and Luke Dillard. Unfortunately for Dillard, the jail cells were not always so empty; he was ambushed by eight inmates in 1901, but he survived a severe beating by the escapees.

Fort Worth's first hospital was founded in 1883 by railroad man J.M. Eddy, who offered $75,000 if the city would provide the land. Citizens raised the $4,000 needed to purchase a site, and a two-story, 300-foot-long frame building was constructed. The structure was first called Missouri Pacific Hospital, but the Sisters of Charity changed the name when it was sold to them in 1889. The last iteration of St. Joseph Hospital, at 1401 South Main Street, was demolished in 2012.

Dr. James Walter Allen (1875–1913) and Dr. Frances "Daisy" Emery Allen (1876–1958) stand ready with doctor's bags. Dr. Daisy was the first woman doctor in Fort Worth and the first woman to receive a medical degree in Texas after graduating cum laude from Fort Worth University's medical department in 1897.

Fort Worth's first mayor (1873), Dr. William Burts (1827–1895) gave the site of his home on Second and Commerce Streets for a fire station and city hall. This second Fort Worth Fire Station No. 1 on that site was designed by Sanguinet & Staats and built by Samuel Tomlinson in 1907. The station served the northern part of downtown until 1980, when it underwent restoration as part of City Center Development by Bass Enterprises.

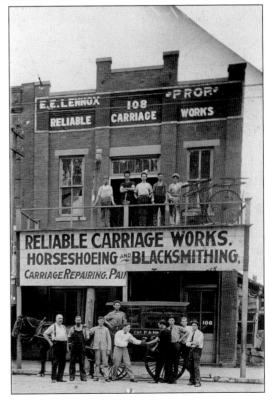

Men pose in front of the Reliable Carriage Works building at 108 North Rusk (now Commerce) Street. Proprietor Edgar Lennox (1859–1925) is buried in Pioneers Rest Cemetery. Like many of the early town leaders, he was a Mason. The street name Rusk had a bad reputation, due to its association with "Hell's Half Acre." The name was changed to Commerce following a petition by business owners in 1909.

Local interests invited Boston capitalist Greenleif W. Simpson to visit with the hope that he would invest. He and a half-dozen associates incorporated the Fort Worth Stock Yards Company in West Virginia because of more favorable tax laws and purchased both the Union Stock Yards and the Fort Worth Packing Company in 1893. A neighbor of Simpson's in Boston, Louville V. Niles, bought half the shares. In 1911, when Fort Worth planned to annex the district, the stockyard interests incorporated as a small community, Niles City, which lasted as a separate entity until 1922. Also shown are the Chicago, Rock Island and Pacific Railway cars near animal pens at the stockyards in the early 1890s when Fort Worth Packing Company opened under local control.

In 1905, when this photograph was taken, the beautiful Mission-style Livestock Exchange was only two years old. While the livestock commission companies are gone, the structure continues to house offices as well as the Stockyards Museum and serves as the central jewel of the Fort Worth Stockyards Historic District.

In this rare photograph, a horse-drawn cart parks in front of the City Hotel. On the back is written, "Mama & Papa Baygents, Irene (in doorway), Myrtie (on post) & Willie; Mrs. McClain in buggy (Mattie is Lou Bowmer's mother), My 1st cousin, T. I. Courtright Stayed here in June 1885." Timothy Isaiah Courtright (1845–1887), first city marshal of Fort Worth, who later ran a protection racket, was gunned down by Luke Short the night of February 8, 1887, following an altercation at the White Elephant Saloon. Courtright had called Short out to the street, where Courtright unexpectedly met his demise. He is buried in Oakwood Cemetery.

Billie Bowman poses during cool weather with his two horses hitched and ready. Bowman and his team helped residents move furniture and goods. His wagon was also ready for service as transportation for picnics and other festive occasions. The cart says "Moving" in large letters below and "Picnic Party Wagon" above. James T. Bowman is listed as a teamster as early as the 1878 city directory. Below is the Southside Livery Stable and Fire Hall at 413 Fulton Street. William E. Mayfield and Robert W. Alvord, proprietors, are listed in the 1896 directory.

This extremely rare interior photograph shows the 1890 Fort Worth High School, on the corner of Hemphill and West Daggett Streets. Public schools, first established in 1882, used rented or donated buildings; when this three-story jewel, designed by Haggert & Sanguinet, was built at a cost of $75,000 as the first public high school, it was the pride of Fort Worth. Tragically, it burned to the ground. A new high school was already under construction on South Jennings Avenue and opened in 1911.

"Dr." Elisha P. Brown, medicine manufacturer, lived and worked on the southside, at 924 Travis Avenue, but sold to towns throughout the area. His festive and musical traveling medicine show is seen on the east side of the 1895 courthouse. The horse fountain, which still stands, is visible behind the wagon.

Pres. Theodore Roosevelt (1858–1919) came to town in April 1905, drawing massive crowds hoping to catch a glimpse of the flamboyant leader. Local photographer C.L. Swartz, with studios at 702 Houston Street, documented the scene in front of the Texas and Pacific Railway Depot.

In this full-length portrait created in 1900 by De Young's Studio in New York City, Harry Longbaugh [or Longabaugh], better known as "the Sundance Kid," and his bride, "Etta," pose as impeccably respectable citizens using the aliases Harry Place and Etta (or Eva) Place. The "Wild Bunch," which included Butch Cassidy and the Sundance Kid, spent time in Fort Worth prior to escaping to South America. Some believe that while "the Kid" was killed in Bolivia, Etta lived the remainder of her long life in Fort Worth. A modern bed-and-breakfast on Third Street named Etta's Place honors the legend.

Fort Worth gained a Carnegie public library, shown in this 1905 Charles Swartz photograph. Built with an 1899 Carnegie grant of $50,000 as well as financing and art donations from the Woman's Wednesday Club, the first building, which included an art gallery, opened in 1901 and stood near the city hall until it was razed in 1937. Architect Herbert H. Green designed the impressive structure.

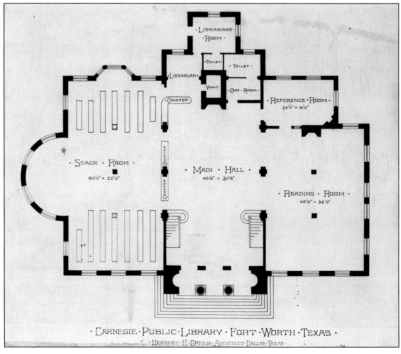

This artist's rendering of the Hoxie Building, later known as the Farmers & Mechanics National Bank, depicts city bustle at the northwest corner of Main and West Seventh Streets. Built in 1889–1890, the eight-story structure was demolished in 1920, and the 25-story building that still stands on that corner was constructed in its place as the downtown skyline grew ever higher. Shortly thereafter, the bank merged with Fort Worth National Bank.

A block or so away was the Harrold Building on the corner of Sixth and Houston Streets. The Fair was an early department store with F.T.B. Schermerhorn as proprietor. At the Fair, a family could purchase everything from children's books to ladies' hats and men's ready-to-wear jackets.

Self-made millionaire and banker William Madison McDonald (1866–1950), who served as Texas Republican Party chairman as well as a national delegate, is shown relaxing at his rolltop desk in a portrait taken by Calvin Littlejohn. "McDonald told blacks that if they wanted their own businesses they should start setting them up," author Reby Cary said. "If you want your own newspaper, you set it up. Don't go around with your hat in your hand asking, 'What are you going to give us?'" McDonald's grand home at 1201 East Terrell Avenue was unfortunately torn down. He is buried in Oakwood Cemetery next to his wife, Mattie Helen (1878–1926), and son Harry Manack (1903–1930).

Completed in 1889, the impressive Board of Trade Building stood on the northwest corner of Houston and West Seventh Streets. Its tower stood seven stories, leading some to call it the first skyscraper in Fort Worth. The post office was housed here until 1896, when a new one was completed on Jennings Avenue. Following numerous calls to do so in the daily newspaper by B.B. Paddock, the Fort Worth Board of Trade began in 1876 in the law offices of John Peter Smith and J.J. Jarvis over Tidball and Van Zandt's bank. The building shown was demolished, leaded-glass windows and all, in the late 1940s. Ladd Furniture & Carpet Company can be seen to the right.

Two men stand at the entrance to Edward Carr's repairing and horseshoeing business at 104 North Rusk (now Commerce) Street. Advertisements hang on the open doors, including one for Lackey's Liver Lifters, which could be obtained at Lackey Pharmacy across from the Texas and Pacific Depot. At least four posters announce shows at the Majestic Theatre.

HOUSTON STREET, SOUTH FROM THIRD STREET.

BLESSING PHOTO
SUPPLY CO.

These two views allow a look up and down Houston Street in 1902. The above view looks south from Third Street, while the below view looks north from Ninth Street. Restaurants, banks, theaters, grocers, dry goods, saloons, barbers, shoemakers, billiard parlors, lodgings, candy shops, cigar stands, leather shops, harness repair shops, photography studios, train ticket outlets, and drug, jewelry, luggage, and clothing stores created a bazaar of businesses, sights, sounds, and smells as people hopped on and off wagons or electric streetcars, or sauntered down the sidewalks.

L. A. Barnes

Railroad tracks leave the T&P passenger station, which can be seen in the distance above. Interurban service between Dallas and Fort Worth by the Northern Texas Traction Company began around the time of these photographs in 1902. George Bishop purchased the City Railway of Fort Worth and the Dallas and Oak Cliff Elevated Railway, then created an interurban line connecting the two cities. Shown below is the freight and baggage terminal at 114 West Belknap Street. The last run of the interurban was in 1934.

Above, the rubble of the Texas and Pacific shops and roundhouse stand silently after burning in 1904. Below, five years later, Fort Worth endured "the great southside fire of 1909." Two boys playing with matches were said to be the cause. The fire, fed by wood-frame, wood-shingled houses and winds gusting to 40 miles per hour on that fateful April day spread with uncontrollable fury. Three historic churches, as well as seven blocks of homes and businesses, were gone. South Main Street looked like a war zone.

Three

FROM FIRE TO FLOOD
1909–1949

Automobile owners gather in the foreground while horses and buggies are in use in front of the Texas and Pacific Railroad station—perfectly symbolizing the revolution in transportation. In the center of it all stands the Al Hayne monument, at 225 West Lancaster Avenue, erected in 1893 by the Women's Humane Association to commemorate the British visitor credited with saving more than a dozen lives in the Spring Palace fire of 1890.

Photographer Lewis Wickes Hine (1874–1940) captured the image and story of Eugene Dalton in 1913: "For nine years this sixteen-year-old has been newsboy and messenger for drugstores and telegraph companies. He was recently brought before the Judge at Juvenile Court for incorrigibility at home. Is now out on parole, and was working again for drug company when he got a job carrying grips in the Union Depot. He is on the job from 6:00 A.M. to 11:00 P.M. (seventeen hours a day) for seven days in the week. His mother and the Judge thinks he uses cocaine, and yet they let him put in these long hours every day. He told me 'There ain't a house in 'The Acre,' (Red Light district) that I ain't been in. At the drug store, all my deliveries were down there.' He says he makes from $15.00 to $18.00 a week." Below, this 1910 view along Main Street looking north from Fifth Street toward the Tarrant County Courthouse shows the town around the same time.

Main Street looking North from 5th Street, Fort Worth, Tex.

With the West Texas oil boom, Fort Worth was in high cotton. By 1910, horses were becoming less common on Main Street, while the number of bicycles, automobiles, and electric streetcars rose. At right, Haltom's is seen before its famous clock was installed. The steel framework for the Burk Burnett building is under construction north of the Fort Worth National Bank. On the far side of the steel frame is the newly completed Westbrook Hotel, which was imploded in 1978 to make room for Sundance Square parking. The 1895 courthouse is visible with the flag atop. Some residents still preferred the horse-drawn carriage. Below, John Wilson stands ready to make rounds for Fort Worth Laundry in 1910.

While talk of a city waterworks began in 1873, funding was lacking. A deadly outbreak of typhoid in 1882 prompted B.B. Paddock and other leaders to create a private waterworks company. Built at the juncture of the Clear and West Forks of the Trinity, it pumped four million gallons a day and soon transitioned to city ownership. This rare photograph discovered by Dalton Hoffman is of that early waterworks. The Holly Pump Station (1892) and Filtration Plant (1911) at 920 Fournier Street greatly increased capacity. That plant was built concurrently with the city's first water supply lake. Lake Worth was first filled in 1914. The "Holly" name for the 1892 plant came from the original pumping engines and boilers, purchased in 1891 from the Holly Manufacturing Company of Lockport, New York.

Founded in 1889, Fort Worth University was in decline in 1910. In 1911, the liberal arts school moved out of state to become part of the present Oklahoma City University. In 1906, ground was secured for a young ladies' boarding school called Arlington Heights College (below), at 4800 Geddes Avenue, near lake Como. In 1910, windmill manufacturer Fred Axtell chaired the board, while an all-woman advisory board included the wives of W.D. Reynolds, Dan Waggoner (Sicily), J.L. Johnson, C.A. O'Keefe, E.E. Baldridge, G.A. Scaling, and Willard Burton. The college lasted only a few years, and may have housed Camp Bowie base hospital staff in 1917.

61

Fort Worth attracted Texas Christian University (TCU) in 1910 by offering a 50-acre campus and $200,000 when fire destroyed the college's main building in Waco. While the new campus was planned and built, TCU held classes in this and other buildings in downtown Fort Worth.

The main entrance on the east side of Our Lady of Victory College and Academy is shown when it opened in 1910. This school moved and was incorporated into the University of Dallas in 1956.

Above, this view looks west along Seventh Street from the corner of Main Street in 1912. The Farmers and Mechanics National Bank is on the right; Ruby Billiards and Pool is at left. Below, the old Fort Worth City Hall with clock tower is shown with the Carnegie library to its right. Ellison Furniture can be seen beyond the clock tower, and the 1895 courthouse is behind it on the horizon. This photograph was taken from the roof of the post office/federal building.

Above, exotic plants create a lush setting for the monument in Peter's Park designed to honor John Peter Smith, a generous benefactor to the city. Catherine Terrell McCartney identified the children on Fort Worth's kindergarten surrey pictured below in 1906: from left to right are Mary Orrick, Louise Hudson, Eugene Orrick, Elizabeth Duringer Gaither, Margaret Hudson, Katie Bowlin Staude, Lillian Morrison, Rebecca J. Morrison, and Chris Hill. Hilda Staude stands at far left, with adults Mother Rintleman, David Stevens, Hardy Anderson, and teacher Katherine Bowlin.

This Fort Worth policeman wearing badge No. 39 had his portrait made at Carter Photography Studio, 206 Western National Bank, at Ninth and Houston Streets. The Fort Worth Police Department started on April 12, 1873, when E.M. Terrell was appointed city marshal with a force of four officers.

In 1889, May Hendricks Swayne (1856–1940) founded the Woman's Wednesday Club in her home at 503 East First Street. As the fifth of 10 children, she was raised during the times of cattle drives into the city, when she and her siblings were made to lie on the floor as a cattle drive went through town so they would not be hit by bullets fired by the drovers. Her husband, John Felix Swayne, served as county clerk and was involved in real estate and the cattle stock market. Both are buried in Pioneer's Rest Cemetery. The club that May founded is the oldest existing club in Fort Worth, and has played a key role in the culture of the city.

1912

Furnished with amenities imported from Europe, the Westbrook Hotel, completed in 1910, was said to be the finest hotel west of the Mississippi. The block between Main, Houston, Third, and Fourth Streets was the site of a hotel for more than a hundred years. In 1877, the El Paso Hotel (C.K. Fairfax, proprietor; Fort Worth City Hotel Company, owner) opened its doors, followed in 1885 by the Pickwick (J.M. Huffington) and in 1895 the Delaware Hotel (M.C. Hurley). Ben Tillar purchased the block in 1898, tore down the old Delaware Hotel by 1909, and in 1910, built the Westbrook, named for his father, J.T. Westbrook Tillar (1833–1908). The Golden Goddess sculpture pictured at left was said to bring luck to oil speculators.

These portraits of Benjamin Johnston Tillar (1866–1923) and Genevieve Eagon Tillar (1874–1961) hang against all odds in the Tarrant County Archives after having been discovered by former archives volunteer Joe Barentine in a California garage in 2013. The Tillars wed in 1898, and first lived at 411 First Street—now exactly underneath where the archives are located. For this reason, it is said that they came home. After moving to Fort Worth in 1894, Benjamin Tillar cofounded Bush and Tillar, which soon became one of the largest beef producers in Texas. He played a major role in the establishment of the National Live Stock Bank. Divesting in 1906, he devoted himself to creating the Westbrook Hotel. Oil was discovered in Electra, Texas, followed by a boom in Ranger. The Westbrook became an important center for West Texas oil and gas transactions. Tillar met an untimely death in Paris. A wing of the Modern Art Museum of Fort Worth is named in honor of the couple.

Mrs. J. Frank Norris's Bible class poses for a group portrait. Her husband, Fort Worth's First Baptist Church pastor, was considered the most prominent preacher in the South. His church has been described as part sanctuary, part circus tent. For example, the pastor once had a washtub full of rattlesnakes brought into the church auditorium to prove that snakes would not harm him. The First Baptist Church later moved from Third and Taylor Streets to Fourth and Throckmorton Streets, as shown below with both cars and horse-drawn carts passing.

Tarrant County Orphan Home, shown above in 1910, was set on 28 acres off Lancaster Avenue and provided food, shelter, and vocational training for some 100 children. Starting in 1887, the Benevolent Home Association cared for local orphans in the Lloyd Building on Main Street and later moved to a home near Samuels Avenue and Cold Springs Road that had previously been a house of prostitution. The 1908 building, shown above, burned in 1914, with the children taking refuge in the 1895 courthouse. Architects Muller and Pollard designed a replacement three-story building, constructed of brick and reinforced concrete. Stop No. 4 on the interurban (below) was convenient for residents taking trips into town.

Off for a Big Time on The Interurban Line between Ft. Worth and Dallas.

In the street view above of Hermann Park and the trolley lines in 1910, repairs after the 1908 flood are visible. Portions of a Gold Medal Beer advertisement on the fence are gone because fence boards had to be replaced. Hermann Park was on North Main Street near the foot of the Paddock Viaduct. The same location is shown below during a flood two years earlier. Gold Medal Beer was manufactured by the local Texas Brewing Company. The park was a favorite meeting place for German immigrants.

The exterior of the Texas Brewing Company and sidewalks lined with trees are shown in the photograph above by L.A. Barnes. Below, a rare interior shot of the bottling room shows employees with beers in hand. Texas Brewing Company built a brewery in 1890 at Jones and Ninth Streets that ran down Jones to Twelfth Street and east to the railroad tracks, where the intermodal station now stands. During Prohibition, the company expanded its cold storage facilities and offered food storage services.

This 1911 view from the top of the Texas Brewing Company showing remnants of Hell's Half Acre in the foreground was the banner image for the sheet music "Panther City March." The Wheat Building dominates the background on the far left, with First National Bank to its right and the Board of Trade between them. The Metropolitan Hotel is in front of the Board of Trade with the Hotel Worth (also seen below, facing Main Street between Seventh and Eighth Streets) in front. The Commercial Club is the peaked shape on the skyline in the center, with the Opera House, Fort Worth National Bank, and Westbrook Hotel to its right. The 1895 courthouse is on the far right.

The old Majestic Theatre (1905–1910) was on Jennings Avenue near Twelfth Street behind St. Ignatius Academy, but the new Majestic (pictured) was at Tenth and Commerce Streets. Theaters of size began with the Fort Worth Opera House built in 1882 by a syndicate headed by Walter Huffman. It struggled to fill its 1,200 seats. Henry Greenwall acquired the opera house in 1890 and sent his son Philip to manage it.

Byer's Opera House is shown just prior to being torn down in 1906. There are two stories: One says that during a production of *Ben Hur*, the horses on the treadmill put too much strain on the stage. Another says that a strong wind blew the building out of line by four inches. It was replaced in 1908 by Byers Opera House, which became the Palace Theater in 1919 when motion pictures began taking over. The Palace was torn down in 1977, but a lightbulb from it still shines in the Stockyards Museum.

Donning large ribbons pinned to their jackets, these men celebrate Labor Day, September 7, 1916. From left to right are H.E.L. Paisley, A.L. Bailey, E. Royer, J. Trout, C.E. Gordon, L. Friedman, H. Andrews, C.E. Head, H.M. Palmer, F.H. Bates, William Lee, L.D. Spranger, S.A. Austin, J.C. Granbury, W.A. Zabel, E. Beam, C.M. Fox, and R.P. Kiesel. The photograph was taken by Bryant Studio, at 705½ Main Street. Also by Bryant Studio is the 1917 image below of Fort Worth Fire Department men and their truck. Unfortunately, the studio burned in 1925 along with thousands of historic negatives.

Hemphill Residences.   FORT WORTH, Texas,

Near Southside residences, such as those seen above along Hemphill Street, proliferated in the early 1900s. Now a solid brick rather than a wood-frame structure, St. Joseph's Infirmary (below) opened a training school for nurses in 1906. Started as a suburb in the late 1800s, the Near Southside is undergoing rapid revitalization. In addition to medical services, cutting-edge entertainment venues, eateries, and residential properties are transforming the historic area.

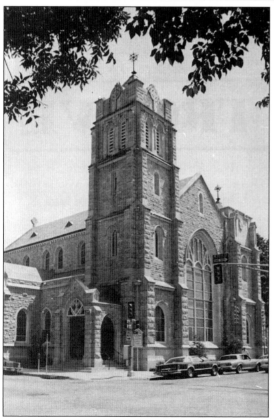

Downtown was not just a place for businesses; it was also where most folks went to church. The above view looks northwest toward the Old Rock Church, the First Christian Church in Fort Worth at West Sixth and Throckmorton Streets. The church was founded by K.M. Van Zandt along with others. Next to the church is the Fort Worth Chamber of Commerce auditorium. Behind the auditorium are the steeples of the First Presbyterian Church on Taylor Street. Shown at left is St. Andrew's Episcopal Church at 901 Lamar Street.

The interior of the coliseum is shown above during the Fancy Stock Show. On the floor of the coliseum are judges seated in the middle, with horses and cattle lined up along either side. Below, the main entrance to the horse and mule area, called "Mule Alley," is pictured. The yards claimed to be "the most modernly equipped buildings, barns, pens and offices in the United States. A great market that has made wonderful growth." C.B. Team Mule Company can be seen on the left.

The Stockyards National Bank, according to its literature, aided materially in the growth of the horse and mule business, with claims that the bank "is ready at all times to further assist in the development of the livestock industry in Texas." An Anchor Fence Company sign and fence are in the foreground, with the *Daily Live Stock Reporter* building at right. The Munn Hotel sign is visible along Exchange Avenue in this view looking west. The Western National Bank (left), at Ninth and Houston Streets, was also active in cattle and oil interests.

Earl Bailey (1892–1918) is pictured as a working cowboy above and a doughboy at right. He spent most of his life on ranches in West Texas before being drafted into the Army in 1918. Bailey had hoped his job in the Army would be to "break broncs," but he was put into the infantry. He trained at Camp Bowie as a private in Company C, 141st Infantry, 36th Division. Bailey died in the bloody Meuse-Argonne Offensive in France, the final engagement of World War I. He was 25 years old. He was posthumously awarded the French Croix de Guerre for heroism. The commendation reads: "A remarkably brave soldier during operation on October 8, 1918, near St. Etienne. He advanced over a terrain swept by a violent bombardment. By his courage, he contributed largely toward neutralizing the fire of the enemy machine guns and destroying their emplacements. Killed during this operation."

More than 5,000 from Fort Worth and Tarrant County served in World War I, with 7,696 Great War veterans buried here. Here, Robert Allen and a young lady stand in front of the log cabin built by his grandparents. The cabin survives today as part of the White Settlement Museum. The Allen family were early pioneers in the Fort Worth area, arriving from Kentucky in 1854. Dr. James W. Allen (see page 42) was from this same family. Seaman 2nd Class Allen served as a radio operator on the USS *McDougal*.

Fort Worth had more aerial training facilities in World War I than any other city in Texas. "Taliaferro" was the British name for the three flight-training facilities set up with Fort Worth as the headquarters. Canadian fliers practiced here until the United States entered the war, when all three were turned over to the US government. Taliaferro No. 1 was Hicks Field (shown), Taliaferro No. 2 was Caruthers, then Benbrook Field, and Taliaferro No. 3 was Everman Field.

Marching south on Main Street, the 36th Division passes in review on April 11, 1918. The unit is also known as the Panther Division or Lone Star Division. The 36th Infantry combat service badge is an inverted arrowhead with the letter *T* for Texas centered within it, indicating that the men were recruited from Texas and Oklahoma / Indian Territory. The unit saw heavy action in France as part of the Meuse-Argonne Offensive, suffering 2,584 casualties. The white-front building is the Odeon Theater. The store fronts of David H. Keene, jeweler, at 1001 Main Street, and Arthur Simon's loan office at 1008 Main Street can also be seen.

The Moslah Shriners began operations in Fort Worth in 1914, rapidly growing to 659 nobles. Requiring a large gathering place, they built this mosque high atop the eastern shore of newly formed Lake Worth in 1917. The site had been known as Reynolds Point, named for cattleman George Reynolds, but ever since has been called Mosque Point, although the structure is gone. Lake Worth was welcomed as a recreational wonder in addition to providing water and flood control for Fort Worth.

A crowded classroom is shown in 1917 at the Colored High School, which is now I.M. Terrell High School, at 1201 East Thirteenth Street. While in Fort Worth training with the Royal Air Force, Canadian William John Connery taught classes and can be seen standing by the door. Isaiah Milligan Terrell (1859–1931) was principal of the school from 1890 to 1915, and the school was renamed in his honor in 1921. The year prior to that name change, the football team and coaches pose in front of the school with a pennant reading "CHS Fort Worth."

The postcard above shows a view of Main Street looking south from the Tarrant County Courthouse. Shown are N.E. Grammer's drugstore, Exchange State Bank, and a sign for Stripling's department store. The Tarrant County Administration Building now stands where the Exchange Bank is shown across from the 1895 courthouse. The same intersection is visible in the photograph below of a man changing lightbulbs on the dome of the courthouse, with the intersection of Main and Weatherford Streets visible below.

Klu Klux Klan Auditorium
Fort Worth, Texas

The Fort Worth Klan No. 101, Knights of the Ku Klux Klan, was begun in 1916. Violent activities included a lynching of a black man accused of killing a police officer in 1920. The group had 6,000 members by 1922. The original klavern on North Main Street was completed, then destroyed—some say by bombing—in 1924. An even larger auditorium seating 4,000 soon stood in its place. In 1931, Leonard's Department Store purchased the building for a warehouse. Later, it was used as a boxing arena, then by Ellis Pecan Company, whose name remains on the structure. The cavernous tan brick building has been vacant for years, and sits on the edge of the new Trinity River Diversion Channel. Shown here is the original klavern.

Following a devastating fire in 1929, the First Baptist Church at Fourth and Throckmorton Streets (see page 68) lay in ruins. Two years prior, pastor and Klansman J. Frank Norris shot and killed lumberman Dexter Elliot Chipps in the church office. Norris was charged with murder but was acquitted on the grounds of self-defense. Neither the scandal nor the fire stunted growth of the church, which boasted 12,000 members and property valued at $1.5 million less than two years later.

Entertainment in the 1920s had a new kid in town—the movies. *Auction of Souls* was the movie playing at the Hippodrome Theatre, at 1106–1108 Main Street, when the photograph above was taken. The film, released in 1919, was based on the book *Ravished Armenia* by Aurora Mardiganian about her experiences in the Turkish genocide of Armenians. While the movies grew in popularity, Fort Worthians continued to enjoy live excitement at the Stock Show and elsewhere. At right, performer Soapy Williams rides a wild bronc named Cox.

The Fort Worth Chamber of Commerce building stood at the southwest corner of Throckmorton and West Fifth Streets. A banner at the entrance reads, "Boys Agricultural, Girls Canning, and Womens Community Clubs Show." The interior photograph below shows a crowd waiting to hear J.W. "Hog Creek" Carruth speak, while a banner on the balcony calls Carruth "The Fortune Maker." Carruth and his Desdemona-based oil company prospered in 1919 by becoming a Ponzi scheme in which Carruth used naïve investors' money to pay dividends, thereby luring more buyers in a spiral that lined his pockets while emptying theirs. He also profited by selling his buyers' personal information on "sucker lists." Indicted in 1923 along with 25 other Texas promoters for fraudulent use of US mails, Carruth was sent to the federal penitentiary in Leavenworth, Kansas, for a year. He died in obscurity in 1932. Later, the Securities and Exchange Commission was established to protect the public from such deceptive stock promotions.

This beautiful vista of Fort Worth Botanic Garden's Rose Garden was the scene of countless weddings and other celebratory events in Fort Worth for decades. Built with some 4,000 tons of Palo Pinto sandstone, the historic shelter house sits high above the rose ramp, providing panoramic views of the reflection pond.

A circus parade heads south on Main Street, with the Tarrant County Courthouse in the background. Businesses include the Southwestern Engraving Company, Busy Bee Café, Fort Worth Army Store, Hotel Worth, Queen Theatre, Denver Theatre, and the Quong On Café, as well as the Whitefield Room and Wolf & Klar pawnbrokers.

In this rare photograph, police officer Joe V. Graham poses with his wife, Pearl, in 1926. Officer Graham died at age 38 from an infection incurred in the line of duty. Graham was on his way home one day in 1935 when he was involved in a car accident at Twenty-Fifth and Market Streets. He noticed that the other driver was intoxicated and told him he was under arrest. The man bit Graham on the tip of his right middle finger. Graham completed the arrest but died later and was buried in Mount Olivet Cemetery. He had been with the department for nine years.

On September 26, 1927, Lindbergh Day was celebrated at Meacham Field. Above is an aerial view of Meacham Field including the airplane hangar and surrounding area. Two images overlay the original photograph of Meacham Field: a portrait of Charles Lindbergh and the *Spirit of St. Louis*. The photograph is by Casino-Hollywood Studio of Lake Worth. Below, this aerial view looks north from between Main and Commerce Streets at downtown Fort Worth and shows the courthouse in the background; it was taken on May 28, 1928.

The world's first helium plant, shown here in 1927, was operated by the US Navy to fill its airships. Fort Worth's helium plant had its origin in a World War I–era experimental helium-extraction station. On December 4, 1917, the *Dallas Morning News* reported that a "chemical plant" was being built near north Fort Worth. For the sake of national security, the plant was kept secret and guarded by soldiers from Camp Bowie. The dirigible gas bags were made from laminated sheets of cow intestine obtained from the Fort Worth packing plants. By 1924, workers added a mooring mast so dirigibles could refuel directly. Several of the buildings remain. Below, the Navy dirigible *Los Angeles* floats over the newly constructed Montgomery Ward Building on its way from the Panama Canal Zone in September 1928. The vessel was acquired from Germany as war reparations following World War I.

Above, in a portrait of the prosperity in 1928, just prior to the tremendous slam of the financial crash of 1929, customers eagerly await the opening of the Fort Worth Montgomery Ward department store on West Seventh Street. The dedication plaque read, "Erected by Montgomery Ward and Company for and dedicated to the constant service of the people of the great southwest whose patronage since the company was founded in 1872 has made this building possible." The interior included resplendent Spanish décor, such as dramatically lighted balconies with carved wooden columns and stenciled beams, or *vigas*. The building (below), which has withstood floods and tornados, has been repurposed as shops, restaurants, and residences.

Fort Worth's Masonic Home and School of Texas was a home for widows and orphans from 1889 to 2005 and now functions as a charter school. Starting in 1913, it had its own school system, the Masonic Home Independent School District. The campus, located in the area roughly bounded by East Berry Street, Mitchell Boulevard, Vaughn Boulevard, Wichita Street, and Glen Garden Drive, included buildings designed by architects Wiley G. Clarkson of Fort Worth, and was listed in the National Register of Historic Places as the Masonic Widows and Orphans Home Historic District in 1992. It is perhaps most famous as the home of the Depression-era football powerhouse known as the "Mighty Mites."

Above, the audience observes in rapt attention as the Queen of the Horse Show is presented inside the North Side, or Cowtown, Coliseum on Exchange Avenue as part of the 1928 Fort Worth Stock Show. At right, a trick rider is shown with her husband and son standing in front of the Stock Show's emergency hospital in 1930. The hospital was donated by the *Fort Worth Star-Telegram*, and all staff were volunteers. The first Fort Worth Stock Show took place on the banks of Marine Creek in North Fort Worth by 1896, but from 1908 through 1944, it was held in the coliseum shown above. After that, the show moved to the Will Rodgers Coliseum in the cultural district until 2019.

The transportation scene was changing in Fort Worth as in the rest of the nation as gas stations, bus stations, and motor lodges proliferated along with vast stretches of paved roads where once there had been only dirt. Above, the Hostetter brothers pose next to their gas pump while a driver stands next to a vehicle in front of Hostetter's paint, garage, and body works and Sinclair gasoline station at 5013 East Lancaster Avenue. Bowen's Bus Center, which included a hotel and drugstore, is shown below.

Clota Terrell Boykin was a local and statewide leader in the woman's suffrage movement. As a delegate from Tarrant County, she served as one of the first women elected to a statewide party convention. Her home during those years, 1709 South Adams Street, which she shared with attorney husband Stanley Boykin and daughters Clota and Camilla, still stands in the Fairmount National Historic District. Her golden "Votes for Women" ribbon adorns the inside front of her scrapbook, which she kept from 1915 through 1930. The scrapbook covers the successful attainment of women's right to vote in Tarrant County and Texas, the successful passing of the Nineteenth Amendment in 1920, and the subsequent early participation of women as they became more directly involved in the political process, supported by the League of Women Voters.

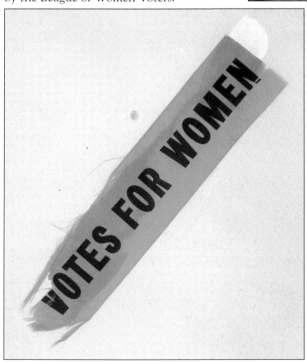

Two Fort Worth Fliers are shown making a refueling test over Fort Worth Municipal Airport (Meacham Field) in 1931. An innovative refueling hose, visible extending from the bottom of the upper plane, was first tested in Fort Worth several years earlier by Reginald L. Robbins and James H. Kelly, which won them the world's endurance flight record in 1929. The refueling ship accompanied the *Fort Worth* to Nome, Alaska, for final refueling.

Pictured here is a rare image of the Fort Worth Stock Yards during a typical workday in the 1930s.

Monnig's Department Store began in 1890 on the 1200 block of Main Street, then moved in 1925 to Fifth and Throckmorton Streets; it expanded to cover the entire block by 1950. Dr. Oscar Monnig and Hugo Monnig migrated from Rees, Prussia (now Germany), in the 1840s, settling in Missouri. Selling their store there in 1889, they moved to Fort Worth. Monnig's, the last of the locally owned downtown department stores, closed in 1990. The 1930s display window above shows an elegantly attired mannequin advertising "The Season's Most Important Sports-Wear Occasion"—the Arlington Downs horse race. Below is an Easter display at The Fair department store.

Originally the Fort Worth Panthers, the Fort Worth Cats were a minor-league baseball team that mostly played in the Texas League from 1888 through 1964. The Panthers had a winning streak from 1919 to 1925, when they won the regular season title seven years straight. They were again league champs in 1937 and 1939, when this photograph was taken. LaGrave, the Cats' home field, was east of North Main Street between downtown and the stockyards.

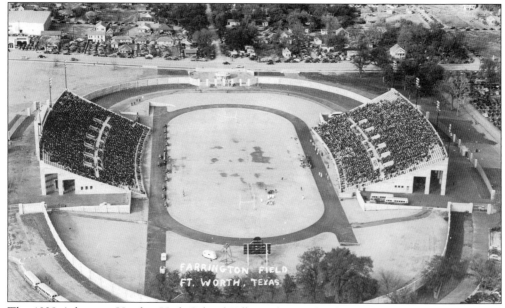

The 1938 Arlington Heights High School *Yellowjacket* yearbook was dedicated "to the revered memory of the late E.S. Farrington, who for many years devoted his time and interest to high school athletics, and who made possible the construction of the new football stadium." Farrington Field, on the corner of University Drive and Lancaster Avenue, remains in use today.

On July 4, 1935, Joe T. Garcia and family opened this tiny restaurant on the north side that would grow into a Fort Worth institution. It has been said that a visitor has not made a trip to Fort Worth unless they have eaten at Joe T.'s. Joe ran a meat business prior to opening the restaurant, but as his wife's cooking grew in fame, "Mama Sus," who hailed from Michoacán, Mexico, used her skills and family recipes as the basis for the new business.

The sisters of St. Mary of Namur ran the San Jose School on the Northside. Shown is the 1949 championship San Jose football team.

Above, installation of super-modern fiberglass and steel walls is shown in the 1940 construction of the Fort Worth Aircraft Assembly Plant. Built for the War Department by the Army Corps of Engineers, it was where the B-24 Liberator soon rolled off the lines. With the start of World War II, the French ordered 60 aircraft sight unseen from Consolidated Aircraft, followed by Britain and later the United States placing far larger orders. Today, with a staff of some 17,000, the site is where the F-35 Lightning II Joint Strike Fighter is produced by Lockheed-Martin. The striking modernity of the plant contrasts with the many older repurposed buildings around town at that time. Shown below is the old First Presbyterian Church at the corner of Fifth and Calhoun Streets repurposed as a U.S. Royal Farm Tire Store.

Both the name and the concept of the Washateria started in Fort Worth. Opened on April 18, 1934, Claude and Gladys Tannahill, of 1705 East Vickery Street, allowed people to bring clothing in to wash themselves for an hourly charge. Women with children stand at tables equipped with water hoses, scrub boards, clothes wringers, and four wash tubs. Some 35,000 laundromats are in operation today in the United States, generating more than $5 billion in revenue each year.

The entrance to KTAT radio station's broadcasting facility on the Denton Highway is seen here as three men finish construction. Arthur B. Tinsley served as plant engineer from 1929 through at least 1937. KTAT was run by Tarrant Broadcasting Company. Raymond E. Buck was president, with offices in the Texas Hotel.

This World War II parade was photographed from the intersection of Eighth and Houston Streets facing north as tanks and military personnel proceed under a banner that reads "Let's Finish the Job."

Fort Worth's Harold L. Valderas trained at Hicks Air Field. This portrait of him in aviator gear was taken in September 1942. Valderas achieved the rank of lieutenant colonel. In later years, he served as district judge of the 233rd Court in Fort Worth. As in World War I, Fort Worth played a significant role in World War II, with a strong presence in aircraft manufacture and training facilities, as well as a massive Army quartermaster depot.

The Paddock Viaduct, named for B.B. Paddock, is shown just prior to the 1949 flood. The 1914 bridge was the first in the nation to use self-supporting, reinforcing steel. Built in 1912, Texas Electric Service Company's smokestacks are on the left. This plant, once key to city growth, is now owned by Tarrant County College.

A rare snowstorm hit Fort Worth in 1948. At left is the 1896 federal building/post office built of rusticated Pecos sandstone. It met the wrecking ball in 1963 to make room for a parking lot. On the right is the city hall built in 1938 by the Public Works Administration and designed by Wyatt Hedrick. Now, it serves as the municipal Public Safety and Courts building, at 1000 Throckmorton Street.

While deluges occurred in 1889, 1908, and 1922, it was the flood of 1949 that brought cries of "enough is enough," resulting in the system of channelization, dams, and levees Fort Worth has today. May 17, 1949, saw muddy waters lapping near the second story of the Montgomery Ward building at 2600 West Seventh Street. Below, an employee indicates the waterline above his head on the first floor. Red Cross estimates reported 13,000 people homeless, with some wooden homes lifted from their foundations and floating downriver. Nine people died, and drinking water had to be trucked in.

Four

FROM FLOOD TO FURY
1949–2000

The 7th Street Theatre, at 3128 West Seventh Street, had been open for less than a year when the 1949 flood inundated it. The classic neighborhood theater with its grand marquee continued operations into the 1990s, when it met the wrecking ball. Its address is now the location of Eddie V's, across the street from the Modern Art Museum of Fort Worth.

This aerial view shows the classic Mid-Century Modern American Airlines Stewardess College among the live oak trees that still surround it. The American Airlines hangar can be seen at top left, and Greater Southwest International Airport, Amon Carter Field, at top right. Built in 1957 as the first flight attendant training school in the world, and now called the American Airlines Training Center, the beautiful building is, at this writing, scheduled for demolition. The airline plans to preserve the iconic stairway where many generations of graduation photographs were taken, in its museum named for founder C.R. Smith.

Phillip Sanders takes a turn on the miniature boat ride in Dixie Park in 1959. The pool was closed in 1960, and the park was sold in 1962. Late 1950s city directories claimed Fort Worth offered more park area per capita than any other city in the nation—4,856 dedicated acres.

This once popular swimming pool in Forest Park was touted as one of the most beautiful in the Southwest and open to the public most of the year. In the South, cities closed public pools such as this one instead of allowing mixed-race use during the 1960s.

The Cowtown Drive-In, at 2245 Jacksboro Highway, opened in 1950 with Gregory Peck in *The Gunfighter*. The iconic mural shown here was not the only local flavor at the 950-car facility; patrons were served by cowgirls dressed in Texas regalia. The drive-in finally turned off the lights in the 1980s. The marquee touts *Stars in My Crown* (1950).

Men and boys shop for model airplanes and boats at Tolson's Hobbycraft on Main Street. Building such models together was a popular father-son activity in the 1950s.

Visitors to Fort Worth enjoyed a new kind of hotel experience at the Western Hills Hotel, replete with its mid-century design and welcoming swimming pool area with striped umbrellas. The hotel, at 6451 Camp Bowie Boulevard, offered 200 rooms, convention facilities, and cabanas that created the illusion of an island retreat.

While author John Griffin (1920–1980) reads the good news about the sudden return of his eyesight, the front page highlights racial violence. Griffin exposed racism in *Black Like Me* (1962) and is buried in Mansfield, south of Fort Worth. In September 1956, a roving band of white youths threatened an African American family who moved into the then all-white Riverside neighborhood. A brave Lloyd Austin held off some 200 demonstrators with a rifle while attempting to protect his family and new home.

Built in 1938, the Dr. Pepper Bottling Company Fort Worth plant, at 1401 Henderson Street, featured a clock and bell tower with the numerals 10, 2, and 4. The bells chimed at those hours, reminding those in town that it was time for a "Pepper-upper." Today, the building houses Trinity Pain Management Associates. Shown here in 1952, the plant continued producing the favored beverage of Texas teens. Dorothy Evans, seen at left in a portrait by her friend Diane McFarland in 1952, was certainly familiar with the sugary brew.

Named for the beloved cowboy humorist, Will Rogers Memorial Coliseum hosted Fort Worth's Southwestern Exposition and Livestock Show until 2019 and was long considered one of the nation's finest equestrian centers. The Will Rogers (1879–1935) statue entitled *Riding into the Sunset* was gifted by Amon Carter and unveiled by President Eisenhower in 1947.

Built on 4.5 acres in 1974, and designed by noted architect Philip Johnson, the downtown Fort Worth Water Gardens was also a gift to Fort Worth by the Amon G. Carter Foundation. Part of the 1976 film *Logan's Run* was shot at this location.

Opened on October 4, 1972, Fort Worth's Kimbell Art Museum, designed by Louis I. Kahn, is widely recognized as one of the most significant works of architecture of recent times. It is especially noted for its silvery natural light that washes from its vaulted gallery ceilings. The skylights use reflectors to spread light across the gallery ceilings. Velma and Kay Kimbell established their art foundation in 1936.

One of Fort Worth's most famous citizens was pianist Van Cliburn (1934–2013), who first achieved worldwide recognition when he won the inaugural International Tchaikovsky Competition in Moscow in 1958. Cliburn's piano-teacher mother discovered him playing at age three. Archives donor Larry Reynolds attended Fort Worth's first Van Cliburn Piano Competition on October 6, 1962, then pinned this autographed program to his wall for daily inspiration as he studied piano. Below is Reynolds's grandfather J.W. Nichols in 1961—still driving his 1901 Oldsmobile.

In March 1962, the vast Seminary South Shopping Center held its grand opening as the first suburban shopping mall in Fort Worth. Entertainment reporter Bobbie Wygant, pictured below, spent all 64 years of her broadcasting career with NBC 5 in Fort Worth. A key feature of the mall was its many fountains. Two nights before Christmas 1974, three teenaged girls went shopping at the center and were never seen again.

Willie Nelson was featured on television's *Cowtown Jamboree* in 1963; the show was recorded live at Panther Hall, at 600 South Collard Street. Bill and Corky Kuykendall opened the 32,000-square-foot bowling alley in 1961, but it soon transitioned to a music venue. *Cowtown Jamboree*, featuring a lineup of popular country artists, aired Saturday evenings on KTVT-TV Channel 11. While Panther Hall, which closed in 1978, helped put Fort Worth on the honky-tonk map, Billy Bob's Texas, 2520 North Commerce Street, brought global recognition as the world's largest nightclub. Billy Bob's, shown below in 1981, covers three acres and features live music as well as live bull riding by top names and is billed as the world's largest nightclub.

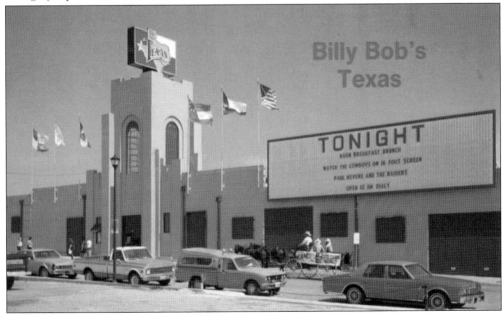

Leonard's Department Store's M&O subway cars transported customers underground from free parking along the river to the suite of stores based around Second and Taylor Streets. This private rail, an innovative concept at the time, ran from 1963 until 2002, surviving the transition of Leonard's to Tandy Center in 1974 but not the transition from Tandy Center to City Place. Leonard's included 83 departments as well as separate grocery and farm implement stores, a cafeteria, a soda fountain, and a service station. Lovingly restored M&O railcar *Leonard's Number 1* resides in the lobby of One City Place, at Second and Throckmorton Streets.

John F. Kennedy spent his last night at the Hotel Texas in Fort Worth, proceeding after addressing a large breakfast crowd in the ballroom to his last moments in Dallas. Thousands of spectators joyfully greeted the president and first lady despite rain. Now the Hilton Fort Worth, the Hotel Texas, designed by Sanguinet & Staats in 1920, is listed in the National Register of Historic Places. A bronze statue of JFK now graces Worth Square across the street from the hotel.

In 1966, as the nation turned to space for inspiration, the 32-foot-long *Challenge of Space* mural by artist Seymour Fogel was installed in the federal office building at 819 Taylor. Numerous other murals dating from the 1930s through 2000 can be found throughout the city.

Founded in 1909, the Fort Worth Zoo received a special gift in 1966: baby elephant Shanti from the Rajah of Kollengode, India. Named by the rajah's children, "Shanti" means peace.

On January 29, 1978, the Westbrook Hotel, at Fourth and Main Streets, was imploded. Legal secretary Christie Smith captured the moment from her office in the Sinclair Building at Fifth and Main Streets. Many boxes of records saved from the Westbrook are now housed in the Tarrant County Archives. Among these is a guest card signed April 20, 1956, by Elvis Presley. His room rate was $4. Below is the Delaware Hotel, which was demolished in 1909 to make way for the Westbrook. A hotel has stood at that location for more than a hundred years, starting with the El Paso Hotel in 1877.

Completed in 1980, Heritage Park Plaza was designed by landscape architect Lawrence Halprin. It is located near the courthouse along the Trinity River. The maze of concrete walls and water features on the original site of the 1849 fort fell into such disrepair that it closed in 2007. Restoration plans are underway. Also seen is the confluence of the Clear Fork (left) and West Fork, with Tandy Center parking along the Clear Fork. The 1911 Criminal Courts building is in the left foreground, and the Texas Electric Service Company power plant is at far right.

The 1990s saw women elected to the highest roles in local government for the first time. First woman mayor Kay Granger (b. 1943) was elected in 1991 and continues in public service representing the Twelfth Congressional District since 1996. Dionne Bagsby (1936–2019) was the first woman and first minority Tarrant County commissioner, serving from 1989 to 2005.

The Bass brothers—Sid, Edward, Robert, and Lee—inherited a fortune from their oil-tycoon uncle Sid Richardson (1891–1959) and have been building on it ever since, while contributing greatly to the reason Fort Worth residents boast to those in Dallas that "our billionaires are better than your billionaires." Shown is the original location of the White Elephant Saloon on Main Street in 1979, after historically sensitive renovation. Bass Enterprises employed architect David M. Schwarz to transform its blocks of downtown Fort Worth. Schwarz soon became the go-to firm for projects across the city, including Sundance Square Plaza, Dickies Arena, Lon Evans Correctional Center, Tarrant County Family Law Center, and many more, creating a distinctive Fort Worth style.

Designed by Wyatt Hedrick and built on three acres in 1931, the Fort Worth Post Office at 251 West Lancaster Avenue is an architectural treasure. As the need for such large downtown post offices diminishes, finding economically viable uses for the 189,000-square-foot Beaux-Arts beauty is key to its survival. Inside, stunning marble columns and architectural details complement the Cordova stone exterior.

The Nancy Lee and Perry R. Bass Performance Hall opened on the corner of Fourth and Calhoun Streets in May 1998. Two years later, an F3 tornado struck downtown. At least 26 city blocks were closed to both pedestrian and vehicular traffic. Almost all entertainment venues cancelled performances, but the Fort Worth Symphony Orchestra continued at the Bass as scheduled. The hall, which seats 2,056, features two 48-foot-tall heralding angels carved into the Texas limestone of its facade.

On the evening of March 28, 2000, Reata Restaurant, then located on the top floor of the Bank One Tower, had the best view of the approaching tornado. When the sirens sounded, 110 customers and 50 staff all safely huddled in the stairwell thanks to fast-acting staff.

Before information was stored in the cloud, the greatest loss besides lives in a downtown hit by a tornado was documentation. Photographs from US Representative Kay Granger's office were found some 20 miles away. Sales tax receipts from Cash America ended up in Meadowbrook. Hundreds of attorneys lost all their case files. Family photographs from Linwood were found in front of the Tim Curry Criminal Justice Center. The loss of original artwork and historic artifacts was extensive.

On the east side of downtown, an area not so hard-hit by the 2000 tornado, Mexican Inn Number One, at Fifth and Commerce Streets, and Barnes & Noble Booksellers stand on the corner with the Bass Performance Hall. Below, true to Fort Worth's "Where the West Begins" motto, a party of six rides along the Trinity. As all good stories must come full circle, across the river on the right below is the very location where the fort began in 1849.

BIBLIOGRAPHY

Cuellar, Carlos E. *Stories from the Barrio: A History of Mexican Fort Worth*. Fort Worth, TX: Texas Christian University Press, 2003.

Chapman, Arthur. *Out Where the West Begins: And Other Western Verses*. New York, NY: Houghton Mifflin, 1917.

Chapman, Arthur, and Estelle Philleo. "Out Where the West Begins." Chicago, IL: Forster Music, 1920.

Freeman, Brevet Lt. Col. W.G. *Inspection of the 8th Military Department*. Washington, DC, 1853.

Garrett, Julia Kathryn. *Fort Worth: A Frontier Triumph*. Fort Worth, TX: Texas Christian University Press, 1996.

Gilson, Margaret M. "A History of the Texas Electric Railway, 1917–1955." MA thesis, North Texas State University, 1972.

Hammond, William Jackson, and Margaret F. Hammond. *La Réunion, a French settlement in Texas*. Dallas, TX: Royal Publishing, 1958.

Haynes, David. *Catching Shadows: A Directory of Nineteenth-Century Texas Photographers*. Austin, TX: Texas State Historical Association, 1993.

Jones, Jan. *Renegades, Showmen & Angels: A Theatrical History of Fort Worth 1873–2001*. Fort Worth, TX: Texas Christian University Press, 2006.

Kline, Susan Allen. "Fort Worth High School." National Register Nomination. 2002.

Knight, Oliver. *Fort Worth: Outpost on the Trinity*. Norman, OK: University of Oklahoma Press, 1953.

McGown, Quentin. *Historic Photos of Fort Worth*. Nashville, TN / Paducah, KY: Turner Publishing, 2007. (Also recommended are other books by this author.)

Nichols, Mike. *Lost Fort Worth*. Charleston, SC: The History Press, 2014. (Also recommended is his history blog, "Hometown Handlebar.")

Newcomb, W.W. Jr. *The Indians of Texas*. Austin, TX: University of Texas Press, 1961.

Paddock, B.B. *Early Days in Fort Worth*. 1906.

Pate, J'Nell. *Livestock Legacy: The Fort Worth Stockyards 1887–1987*. College Station, TX: Texas A&M University Press, 1988.

———. *North of the River: A Brief History of North Fort Worth*. Fort Worth, TX: Texas Christian University Press, 1994.

Perkins, Clay. *The Fort in Fort Worth*. Keller, TX: Cross-Timbers Publishing, 2001.

Roark, Carol and Byrd Williams. *Fort Worth's Legendary Landmarks*. Fort Worth, TX: Texas Christian University Press, 1995.

Sanders, Bob Ray. *Calvin Littlejohn: Portrait of a Community in Black and White*. Fort Worth, TX: Texas Christian University Press, 2009.

Selcer, Richard F. *The Fort That Became a City*. Fort Worth, TX: Texas Christian University Press, 1995.

———. *Fort Worth Characters*. Denton, TX: University of North Texas Press, 2009.

———. *Hells's Half Acre*. Fort Worth, TX: Texas Christian University Press, 1991. (Also recommended are other books by this author.)

Sherrod, Katie, ed. *Grace & Gumption Stories of Fort Worth Women*. Fort Worth, TX: Texas Christian University Press, 2007.

Souvenir Program of the Military Review, 36th Division (Panther Division), 1918. Tarrant County Archives.

Tarrant County Archives. www.tarrantcounty.com. 2019.

TSLA Bird's Fort Treaty Ratification Proclamation. 1843. www.tsl.texas.gov/treasures/indians/birds-01.html.

Terrell, Joseph Christopher. *Reminiscences of the Early Days of Fort Worth*. Fort Worth, TX: Texas Printing, 1906.

Wallace, Edward S. "General William Jenkins Worth and Texas." *Southwestern Historical Quarterly* 54, 2 (October 1950), pp. 159–168.

Worcester, Donald Emmett. *The Chisholm Trail: High Road of the Cattle Kingdom*. Lincoln, NE: University of Nebraska Press, 1980.

Youngblood, Dawn. *The SMS Ranch*. Charleston, SC: Arcadia Publishing, 2017.

Discover Thousands of Local History Books Featuring Millions of Vintage Images

Arcadia Publishing, the leading local history publisher in the United States, is committed to making history accessible and meaningful through publishing books that celebrate and preserve the heritage of America's people and places.

Find more books like this at · www.arcadiapublishing.com

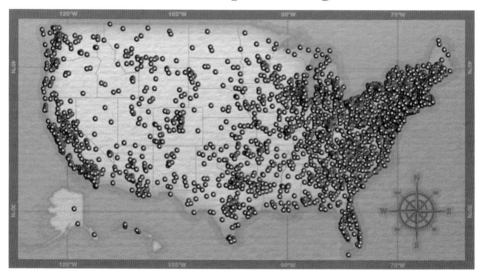

Search for your hometown history, your old stomping grounds, and even your favorite sports team.

Consistent with our mission to preserve history on a local level, this book was printed in South Carolina on American-made paper and manufactured entirely in the United States. Products carrying the accredited Forest Stewardship Council (FSC) label are printed on 100 percent FSC-certified paper.

MADE IN THE USA